Blue Lawn
&
Collide

Blue Lawn

&

Collide

Back together again for the first time

L.E. HASTINGS

Rev. date: 02/25/2013

To order additional copies of this book, contact:
Xlibris Corporation
1-888-795-4274
www.Xlibris.com
Orders@Xlibris.com
126502

Contents

The House onBlue Lawn

When Life&Reality Collide

For my Friends
&
Yard-Sailing Zombies

Also by L.E. Hastings

*Forthcoming

Foreword to Blue Lawn & Collide

The need for republishing these two books was born of the hope that new readers would have the chance to read my earlier works and those that have read these short stories the first time will come back and enjoy them again.

There have been some changes within a few of the stories.

As I've learned more—so too has my writing.

Those few stories that have changes are only surface changes.

Replacing certain words for a bit more palatable eye.

But ultimately the big reason was that I went to a new publishing company.

Now before I go any farther, there was nothing wrong with my relationship with the previous company. When I was ready to have my third publication done there was—it seemed—a changing of the guards within their structure.

With all the High-Tech that we have at our fingertips today, it was just a simple matter as calling,

e-mailing, faxing, skyping, and even snail mail.

But to my disbelief—no answer.

No hard feelings.

Well at least not now.

But it did force me into that place of un-comfortableness.

One of those places where you have to look around you and say,

"Why should I have to change? Everything here looks fine."

So the search went forward.

Finding a new publisher.

To finding answers within my faith, that God hasn't brought me this far just to drop me on my head.

To having the opportunity to really go through my two earlier works and cleaning up the grammar.

The punctuations.

The mistakes that I didn't catch, see, or understand at the time.

God really does work in our lives, even when I'm not asking or ready or just plain stubborn.

So there you have it—the new and improved volumes of my first two books, reprinted together with a new propose in life.

So to you knew readers, welcome aboard.

And to those that have been down this road with me before,

thanks for coming back again.

Enjoy . . !

Endicott

The House on
Blue Lawn

Preface

Right off I would like to explain my intent on what the word recover or better yet recovery means to me.

We all travel the road of life and sometimes it's a rocky one.

Full of ups and downs.

When we do come across those calamities of distress or misfortune,

we have to learn how to deal with the emotion of the event that's right in front of us at that moment.

The words recover or recovery—however you look at it—a terrible loss,

an extremely serious event or something that will leave a long or lasting effect upon us.

It changes us.

"Time heals all wounds." Some say.

"It's all water under the bridge." They say.

"Don't cry over spilled milk." One says.

"There doing better. But it's going to be a slow road to recover." The Doctor said.

It's not my intention to tell you how one should recover or what to do.

I'll leave that up to the professionals.

There were many people who have helped me on my way and still do.

These short stories are just some of my experiences on my journey so far.

Maybe you'll identify—maybe not.

Mr. Webster's definition on recovery is,

"To get back. To restore. A return to a normal condition."

However we get there, our road is our own.

As one of my friends often tells me in life,
"Suck it up cup cake, could be worse, it could be you."
So I do.
On this trip around the sun . . . .

Side Rails—Please

We all seem to hear,
"Don't drink, go to meetings and get a sponsor."
But what do these things mean?
These short little phrases.
Ask for help.
First thing first.
Think or even K.I.S.S.
Are they just things that people say?
For me—no.
They're not just words—they're tools.
Okay, in the beginning they were to me.
Words that made little to no sense at that time.
My head was like a rock and my mind was mush.
I heard you folks' talk about "The Big Book."
Heck, at the time I couldn't even read a comic book.
But I kept coming.
I didn't drink and I heard these words.
"Keep it simple."
"But for the grace of God."
And they started to stick.
I seemed I still had some brain cells left after all in this rock full of mush.
Today, I thank God for those little phrases that weren't too big for someone like me to remember.
For me today, they are tools.
Tools passed down to me from someone who came before me.

I've heard, "Stay on the beam,
cause when you're not,
you may not know it."
So for me I keep my sponsor on one side,
meeting with all there little phrases on the other.
So when I start to lean from side to side on the beam of sobriety,
I can ask for help.
Help today from my sponsor,
the new friends that I've met in meetings.
To me the tools for staying on the beam is asking for help,
cause sometimes I need my Side Rails—Please . . . .

Under the Orange Roof

It's funny how they said my life would change so much.
I didn't think I would be back here, where I used to drink, that's for sure
and where I drank would still be in my life.
It started years ago come to think of it.
Like all stories, this has a beginning.
It starts really with my father.
My father was a cook. Had been a cook even before I was born.
He's been cooking for so long that there's not a time when I can't remember when he wasn't.
To me it seemed when I was little that my father cooked everywhere.
At work, at home, even the church when they needed someone.
My father was always there.
But one of the places stands out most in my mind, one of my favorite places my father took me to when I was young.
When we first pulled up I could see the blue sides of the building and get this—it had an orange roof.
To me it looked so funny like it should have clowns or something living inside of it.
I remember there was this sign over the top of the roof of this man reaching down to a small child.
It made me think of my father and me.
When we were inside my father and I walked through this dark and smoky room with people sitting and laughing.
"Dad?" I asked.
"Are these the clowns that live here?"

He looked down at me with a smile.

"No son." He said.

He went on saying, "They aren't clowns.

But I think some of them do live here, most of the time." And laughed!

He then brought me in the back where he cooked.

Sat me up on this long bench and told me to stay right there and to be good.

"I'll be right back." He said.

He then gave me this chocolate lollipop.

It had the same man and child on it that I had seen on the rooftop outside.

I was no different than most kids—once done with my treat,

my mind started to wander and the body wasn't too far behind.

I went through the kitchen,

on by the ice cream and soda fountain,

to the room that was dark and to me full of clowns.

It was still dark inside.

Maybe they were sleeping I thought?

But how could that be.

It was sunny and warm outside.

Sometimes I could hear the clowns talking and laughing.

I was still standing there in the smoke—filled doorway when my father found me. Needless to say, he never brought me back there.

He said things to me like, "Not staying put." "Could've of got lost." or "Had I gone outside I've might have been hit by a car."

But that made no sense to me.

All I wanted was to see the clowns again.

Little did I know that years later I'd be one of those clowns?

It seems to me that when I started drinking,

I drank everywhere I could.

But the one place that I seemed to make my home was the same place my father had brought me years ago.

I had found a place where people knew me and I them.

We told stories, laughed at bad jokes.

I even had a couple of beers with my father while my mother was at church.

My father would tell me about when he worked here and how much it had changed since then.

To me, it was just a place that I could go to, have a few drinks in peace.
Talk to some people, laugh when they laughed, and were sad when they were sad.
By then I couldn't feel anything and I didn't know why.
So I would order another drink.
Gone were the memories of my childhood.
It seemed there were times when I would not smile or laugh for days.
When I did, it was hollow and dry.
If I didn't laugh, I've break down and cry.
I was so empty inside and I didn't know why.
So I would order another drink.
It wasn't long after that, that I would find recovery.
I didn't know what else to do by then, but I knew in my heart,
that I'd had enough of living the way I was.
I started to go to meetings.
Even picked up my first 24-hour chip at this place, which is now my home group.
I made coffee and later handed out the same chips that I had picked up years before.
They said things like,
"Keep coming back." And "Don't drink, no matter what."
But the things that I remember the most was,
"Change your playground." And "Clean your house." And "The person who walks in this door has to change."
Well I have changed my playground.
My friends—which weren't many by the end of my drinking and cleaned my house.
I found out that a meeting could start before a meeting and go on well after it in parking lots.
In friends cars going to and from a meeting.
Even at places where they serve coffee late at night.
It wasn't long after I met my sponsor that he asked me out for coffee.
I said, "Sure, where?"
"Get in the car." He said.
"We'll go over there.
There will be other people from the meeting there too."
As we pulled into the parking lot I started to laugh.
My sponsor looked at me and asked, "What's so funny?"

"Here?" I asked.

"This is the place where we're having coffee?"

"Sure is." He said.

"Don't tell me you've never been here before?"

"Oh no." I said.

"I've been here many times, come to think of it."

And laughed again.

So here I sit with my new friends.

Not in the dark room of my childhood filled with smoke and clowns.

But near the soda fountains of my youth.

Telling stories of how it used to be.

How my life has changed so much.

And we laugh.

Here—Under the Orange Roof . . . .

Distance in Our Eyes

Most people—well most,
are not really here.
What I mean is that they are here.
But some are always thinking of someplace else.
I'm definitely one of these people.
Most of my life I've been one.
Not being here kind of person.
Even at a young age I was not where I was supposed to be.
Always thinking of someplace distant.
You can see us when looking around.
Anywhere really.
At work, school, even at the grocery stores.
We are there.
Some of us don't even know we are doing it.
Having that distance in our eyes.
Most of the time when I'm there it takes someone sometimes to ask me
that aged old question,
"What's up?" And I'm back.
Back where I'm supposed to be at that moment in time or place.
I've gotten better over the years though.
Better at being where I'm supposed to be but still there are times when,
You can almost imagine that you're there.
Most of the time for me it's not even a place, but a time.
Now I'm not talking about time travel or some silly thing like that.
But mind travel.
Thinking ahead.

Simple really.

Like waiting in line to pay for my gas and my mind takes off to think how badly the bank lines are going to be,

or what I'm going to have for supper tonight.

We're that type of person;

When we see each other we nod.

We enter a room or a place and we usually spot one another.

No words are even spoken between us;

We just nod at each other.

Why would we—we know?

We can see the distance in their eyes.

Some—well most, are so far ahead that they lose track of time.

Always in such a hurry and rush but end up being late anyway.

And then there are those who are looking back, thinking of a time long ago.

Lost in the world that changed so quickly that for some it's unbearable.

It's all the same really.

Past.

Future.

Not being there and I have to be mindful.

Not to step too far behind and live in regrets

or relive those happy times.

Just a short stay.

Never too far ahead.

Being so impatient that I'm lost in my own thoughts.

Losing time.

Talking to us usually helps.

But I know for me even when someone is speaking either to me

or at a meeting I can be looking right at the person and I'm not there.

I'm there but my mind is off somewhere else.

So when we see one another,

we know.

We see it in our eyes.

If you're around many people in many places you'll see us.

Some don't even know.

Just look for those people that nod.

We're everywhere.

We usually have it.

That Distance in Our Eyes . . . .

S.P.A.M.

Spam,
the word just sounds funny.
Like someone forgot to add more letters or just stopped short of the pronunciation of the word.
But Spam stuck.
Simple People Are More.
Simple in their ways, people that move, are willing to go and are more full of life.
Spam,
the word just sounds funny.
It wasn't long after coming into recovery that I thought of Spam.
You see, Spam and I go way back.
Even before I drank, Spam was there.
Not that we were poor, but we weren't rich either.
When I was young Spam was cheap, too cheap if you ask me.
But nevertheless we had Spam.
Simple People Are More.
On those early Saturday mornings with my brother as we sat in front of the TV,
seeing our favorite Captain Kangaroo or Box Car Willie show.
You could hear it cooking along with eggs.
The over—powering smell would reach into the living room as we watched the Uncle Gus show.
Dad would call us; Mom would have the table set,
as we would say the our short version of the Lord's Prayer.
"Thank you for this food, Amen."

Then start to eat—our Spam.

As the years went by my life changed.

But through it all it seemed that no matter where I was living or whom living with, we ate Spam.

It seemed that no matter how much I was making at a job—if I would be working that is.

I always would buy Spam.

It was cheap.

Extra cheap when I had help with food donations from the local Churches.

When my drinking was at its' worst and money, if any was going to my habits,

I would always have enough money to buy some Spam.

Long past was the memory of eating Spam at breakfast.

Now it was replaced with eating when I thought I should or just plain remembered to. Even if it didn't stay down—nothing seemed to at that point.

As a matter of fact, one of my past relationships when I was in full form, all we could afford was Spam.

It was a passing joke between us that we could one day write a cookbook on the,

fine art—when cooking with Spam.

Spam on Triscuits, Spam Q, Bars, Baked Spam,

and my all-time favorite, Spam in a Can.

As I started to stay sober things changed.

They had to if I wanted to stay sober.

But it wasn't long before that Spam was back.

I had done a complete one hundred and eighty degrees with my life and started anew. Things started to happen to me, as in the Promises.

Good things, some not so good.

But I stayed sober one day at a time.

Simple People Are More.

Through it all people have come and gone on my path of recovery.

Recovery and the Fellowship have taught me a new way to live without a drink.

Now you must try to understand it isn't like I went out looking for it.

But there it was nevertheless.

One day like any other, I went to the grocery store with money, my own money.

From a job that I have, a job!

Look, I tell you I didn't even have help from the church.

Walking through the store being able to place items in the carriage and there it was, sitting on the shelf.

Just there.

Spam.

So I bought some along with other items before you ask.

When I arrived back home I put my things away, but when I came upon my can of Spam, I left it out on the counter top.

When I would look around my home I would see many things but my eyes would always return to my can of Spam.

Well, that was a few years ago now.

That can of Spam long gone.

But I did save one thing from that little can—the key.

I ended up placing that key on a chain to wear as a necklace.

Not for a fashion statement—although it is kind of cool.

When people see it some ask why, I tell them. Some people don't.

But when I see it one thing stands out from all the rest, one thing that a program of recovery has taught me,

one thing that is evident every time I look at that key.

I never have to live that way again when I was using.

That one simple key is such a reminder to me of all the good things in my life to be grateful for.

And to top it off, I like Spam.

Simple

People

Are

More

The word just sounds funny.

S.P.A.M . . . .

Don't Walk—Run

They say, don't run—walk.
Look before you cross the street.
Hold my hand and stay with me.
Watch where you're going, pay attention and don't run.
But when I started drinking many years ago, that's exactly what I did.
I ran.
My first drink was just like the people around me.
I drank fast and wanted more.
I should have seen where that drink was going to take me.
Seen where I'd end up.
All the places and people I would meet or cross on my path of using.
Always running to my next drink or drug.
Had I held the hand that was given to me by the ones who loved me
when I was so young.
Would I have stayed?
I don't think so for me.
I was always pulling away—Always running.
Finding out what happened to me by other people the next day.
Waking up and saying,
"Where the heck are we now?"
Looking for some clues to what went on around me.
What happened to the last 48 hours?
Oh I love this one, "Where are my shoes?"
Never listening to what people said to me or what went on around me.
Always having to find out the hard way.
People would say things to me like,

"This is great. You should try it."
Or better yet, here's one for the records.
"Don't do that, I've tried, it's just too much."
My reply would be in my actions always.
"What do they know?
Let me in there, and I'll show them."
Head strong and full of hot air.
The outcome would always be the same when I would be looking for
different results.
Broken.
Now I go to meetings.
I work the steps to the best of my ability.
One day at a time.
In all aspects of my life.
I have to.
I talk to my sponsor and take advice freely given to me.
Well, not always as quickly as I should.
But my sponsor is very patient in this.
But I do try.
Keeping it simple for me means,
"Slow down, don't run, but walk."
But I find now in sobriety that sometimes I have to get to a meeting.
To see my sponsor and to tell my home group how I'm doing and what
I'm doing to keep an open mind.
Telling them how I feel.
Knowing I have to get to a meeting because I can't do it on my own.
That's why for me I don't just walk to a meeting, I run.
So if you're anything like me, someone in recovery and you need to get
to a meeting.
Don't Walk—Run . . . .

The Last Son

A while ago I was sitting down by my mom's side.
She was bedridden due to a sickness she had had for many years.
Not a bad night.
No rain, no heat, just a day.
Well it was night and she was dying.
My father and partner were out for a break and it was my turn to watch
over my mom. Watch, like she was some kind of child or something.
My mom was very with it that night while I was there.
We talked and talked.
About everything and nothing really, just talked.
When I was a child.
When she was one.
She had no regrets she told me.
She didn't want any anyway.
"Life is too short." She told me.
"Mom, can I get you anything?"
I asked as I got up from my chair.
"Yes, please, some water would be nice." She had said.
Looking down at my mom I thought,
what a strong person she is.
Dad said early that she didn't know who he was or where she was this
afternoon.
Sitting back down in the chair beside her with her water in my hand I
asked,
"Mom, do you know who I am?"
"Of course, you're my son." She said.

"I have two.
Your brother was my first and you were my last."
We must have talked for hours it seemed.
She told me how proud she was of me.
But that she was proud to have me sober and in recovery.
That the last four and a half years she had her son back in her life.
She told me that she had been praying for me every day that I was out there using.
"Don't use this as a reason to go out and start drinking again." She said to me that night.
Not to go out, I thought.
God, if there was ever one this would be it.
"No mom, I won't." I said.
She took a couple of sips from the glass I was holding up to her lips.
God, please be with my mom, I thought.
My mom used to say, "That life was like a giant book with all the stories already written down.
Stories of those who came before,
stories that are being read right now and still many stories yet to come."
"You know?" She said to me.
"Going to heaven is the biggest classroom of them all.
All our questions will be answered that you asked in life."
As she looked up at me with eyes so clear.
"I'm going to school tomorrow." She said.
"Mom, is there anything else I can get you?" I asked.
"Yes, give me a hug." She said.
So I did.
I sat with her 'til my father and partner came home.
I told them what she had said about tomorrow.
Dad said she's been like that all day with him.
We decided to stay home from work that next day to be with her.
10:43 a.m. my mom had some breakfast.
At 11:30 a.m. she said to us that she loved us.
"What's the weather outside?" She wanted to know.
"It's a great day, Ma" Dad told her.
"A great day to be alive."
11:48 a.m. my mother died with us holding her hands.

Now she knows I thought.
I was the last son she talked to.
The last son to hold her hand.
For the rest of us, all we can do is turn the page.
From the beginning to the end,
she was always with me.
I can't think of a better gift to give my mom,
from her Last Son . . . .

The Chair with the Crooked Leg

Why is it that I always find this chair?
You know the one—when you walk into a place,
anyplace really, we find it.
Some of those places are familiar, some are just not.
But when we finally sit down we find it.
That chair.
It started way back when I was young.
Not feeling like I fit in or something as simple as not paying much
attention to my whereabouts.
Not being where I was inside.
But I always seemed to find it.
You know, come to think about it, every time I go somewhere new,
I'm always on the lookout for this chair.
The way I look at it is
I might as well find it right off the bat.
Because no matter how hard I try to stay away from it, that darn chair
is there.
Walking into meeting, having people look at me,
doing that all so-familiar nod of my head in recognition,
smiling and reaching out my hand.
Saying my hellos and working my way to the back of the room for
some coffee and treats.
But it's there, in the back of my head.
I'm looking.
Sometimes I just don't like to find that chair.
So I start up the aisle smiling and saying, "Hi."

Until I finally come upon a place to sit.
I take off my coat and place it on the back of my seat,
take one final look around to see if anyone is looking
and then I sit right there on that darn chair with the crooked leg.
Because for me I can still feel like a newcomer.
"Just one of those bozos on the bus." They say.
"Doing what was told to me from the very first meeting."
"Don't drink and it will get better."
And it has, a whole lot better.
But it doesn't mean that I can't feel out of place once in a while.
Knowing what to do and what not to do,
can be just as rocky to me.
Sometimes that chair is very still
and then there are those times when it rocks no matter how hard I try
to sit still.
It was said to me by the old-timers that that's just your higher power
shaking you to share.
Share how I was feeling, tell the group that I'm a drunk
and just trying to stay away from a drink one day at a time.
From my first meeting in recovery, it worked.
Raising my hand and asking for help.
You know, sometimes I really didn't like sitting in that chair.
But when I do now.
I tell them how I'm doing,
what I'm doing and that I can't do it on my own.
That sometimes knowing what to do and not knowing can be just as
confusing.
My life is a whole lot better because I'm sober today.
The people and friends I've made in the halls of recovery are always
there.
You'll see,
if you really need to share.
You'll find it—The Chair with the Crooked Leg . . . .

The Tree with One Leaf

There was this tree outside my window that I would always look at.
This tree became a living sign for me by the end of my drinking.
There were a lot of signs along the way.
Some signs I saw and others—well, let's just say for a lack of a better word, we missed each other.
A lot.
But this tree was one of the things right before I came into recovery that I would look at for a very long time.
I would say to myself,
"When the snow melts off the branches, I'll stop."
Stop what I was doing, even when I didn't know at that time that the drink in my hand was the biggest sign of them all.
It was always something else.
Something other than me.
It was things like my relationship wasn't going where I wanted it to go.
Definitely my parents,
or my brothers and all of their stuff.
Or as simple as my favorite Sci-Fi show was a repeat.
But not,
no, never and I mean this.
It was not I.
It was them.
"I'll stop after the snow melts off this here tree." I'd say.
There I was looking out my window at this tree, by now the snow was all but gone.
The signs of spring were well in the air.

Crocuses were poking up and there was a small robin in my tree.

"I'll stop when that robin leaves." I'd say to myself.

But he never did.

He found a comfortable spot and made a nest.

Can you believe that?

This bird stayed right when I thought about stopping.

Now I'll have to wait till he leaves.

There's always something stopping me.

How long can this bird stay, I thought?

The leaves are getting bigger and it's hard to see that robin,

but I know he's there, because I can hear him sing.

As soon as I can't—well, I'll stop.

There were many signs.

I just didn't see them.

My tree had come to full life by now.

The hot summer breeze was coming through my window as I sat looking out

and listening to the neighborhood children playing in the yard next door.

How can they have fun?

Didn't they know how I felt?

"Go home." I'd say to myself.

"I can't hear my robin any more. I'll stop when they go."

By now the colors where changing from the deep dark greens to the fiery reds

and oranges as most of the trees in my neighborhood had.

They seemed to start at the top slowly working their way down with this bountiful of colors.

"I'll stop after they all change." I would tell myself.

My robin had quit the family in my tree now.

He had made his home about halfway up on one of the larger branches.

I could see him again as I sat there in my chair by the window due to the falling of the leaves.

Most of the trees in the neighborhood had changed and lost their leaves by now.

The changing of the seasons was working their way through my life and I still didn't see the signs.

"I'll stop when they all fall off my tree." I'd said to myself.

Sitting in my chair looking out my window watching the clouds slowly move in.

The signs of winter fast approaching.

My robin had moved on and so had his family,
most likely to a warmer place.

My tree was bare now, well, except for a few lingering leaves that seemed to hang on no matter how much the wind blew.

One by one the last of the leaves would fall to the ground—except for one.

Looking out my window at the first snowfall,
gathering on the lawn, slowly covering the small bushes and plants by the side of my home.

Being able to see the small nest that was a home for my robin friend.

Seeing that one leaf still hanging on.

There were many signs towards the end of my drinking,
many signs I just didn't see.

As I sat in my chair with a drink in my hand, looking out at my tree.

The colors were all gone now,
no reds or orange and greens to see.

All but one leaf was left as the snow slowly covered the nest.

"I'll stop." I would say to myself.

As I looked out my window at The Tree with One Leaf . . . .

Life

I really don't know why it's taken so long since my mom passed away to realize one of the things she used to say to people.

"The way you look at death is the way you look at life."

I always thought I'd know what she meant by that, I was wrong.

It's been playing around in my head these last couple of years now about my mom's saying.

So at this meeting a young person shared.

"They say when you hear it, you'll hear it."

So it was meant for me to hear him talking about when he was in jail, his father passed away.

Now I know that I've never been to jail.

That's a yet, if I decide to pick up a drink and my dad is still alive.

But what stopped me in my tracks is how he felt about not being there for his dad.

You see I had the opportunity to be by my mother's side.

To walk through with her, her final moments and it was hard.

One of the hardest things I've ever done in recovery so far.

But I didn't do it alone either.

My dad and partner were with me.

Along with support from the people I've met in recovery.

To finally realize I was looking at death and it hit me when I listened to that young person.

That I was being blessed.

Blessed with the opportunity to be part of my mother's moments.

To see it first-hand.

To know now that my higher power loved me so much,

that he gave me the strength, courage, compassion
and the awareness of the moment, and I feel blessed.
I am blessed.
Here was this young person having a hard time about not being there
for his father.
He felt so bad and messed up about it, that the only thing I could say
was,
"If you truly feel that you are doing the next right thing, your Dad will
know.
That he is with you in so many ways that can't be described.
That in time you will see and hear the answers to your questions.
That your higher power is working and walking with you.
Life is what we do now, at this moment. Be mindful."
I have found that I don't ever have to be alone in this journey for
recovery.
That you are not alone either at this moment in your life.
Then it came out at that moment. I said to him.
"The way you look at death is the way you look at life."
That wasn't me.
That was my mom, my higher power.
Life.
Death.
At that moment, life was good.
And for that, I am blessed.
Any way you look at it,
It's just Life . . . .

Stowaway

When I stop and think of the word, "Stowaway." My mind goes right to the thought of an uninvited guest on board a large ship.

Someone who has hidden themselves well enough not to be seen.

Far enough away that on the outside, people just don't see them.

Hidden away so well that the only time they surface is to see where they are now or where they're going.

Then right back to their little hiding place.

How about the type of stowaway that tries to have a seat on board a train?

Only to be let out at the next train station.

"What do we have here?"

The conductor would say.

"No ticket, no ride." He says.

"You must get off this here train, my little stowaway.

These people have all paid to have a seat on this train.

We'll see what the law has to say." He would add.

As they lead the stowaway from their little hiding place.

So now I'm in recovery and to my surprise I have found my stowaway.

It's not a person per se.

No child hiding in the back of a slow moving circus brigade,

resting their head for their long ride in the back of a large lion's cage.

Although it does hide very well, especially to me it seem at times.

It only rears its head when I'm not on my guard.

I realize that my stowaway is my disease today.

So well hidden in me that I tend not to see or even notice that it's there.

Raising its head to sabotage my surroundings just to feel well.

My stowaway comes out when I'm happy or sad.

Rainy or sunny.

Having money in my pocket or being flat broke.

My stowaway hides in me very well.

In my actions and thoughts like a game of chess, sometimes two steps ahead.

It gets me in my sleep where it tells me what fun we had.

"It's going to be different this time." It says to me.

My stowaway hides very well, very well indeed.

But this is one stowaway I can't let off at the nearest station or call the port authority to have them removed.

To know that my stowaway is part of me.

Living one moment at a time within me.

The longer I stay sober the more my stowaway tries to hide.

So I work at the best of my abilities to find it.

Always finding some new part of myself where my stowaway has hidden itself.

The disease of alcohol is in every aspect of my life.

So must too I work on every aspect.

Using the twelve steps to change.

Reading the big book, having a sponsor and friends.

Going to meetings and making coffee.

Using the tools of the program on uncovering my stowaway one day at a time.

Shining some light in the dark corners where it might hide.

If I'm not able to see it,

I have good friends today that help me look at those parts of my life where my stowaway has hidden itself.

Even if I don't want to.

The way I look at it, my stowaway is going to be on a long ride.

God willing, one day at a time within me.

Who knows, maybe, just maybe I'll shine enough light on all the dark corners of my life to have fully uncovered my stowaway.

But for now I have to be content with the knowledge that it's here

and ask on a daily basis from my higher power,

the strength to see my Stowaway . . . .

The Less—Than Club

Ok, maybe you're just like me—maybe not.
But I'm going to tell you anyway.
"I'm a card-carrying member."
Now, now—let me explain what I mean here.
Well at least to those who aren't card members.
You see, even before I started drinking I felt less than.
Never quite fitting in.
Always feeling not part of.
Being in a crowded room and still feeling alone.
Of course you add that with family and my surroundings that said things like,
"Why start that? You'll never finish it."
Or, "Why bother?
Stand up straight.
Look at me when I'm talking to you."
Oh, here's one for the records.
"Because I said so, that's why!"
What the heck did that ever mean anyway?
Then I found alcohol and all that went away.
Well, at least on the surface it did.
I took all those inadequacies,
mixed some booze into the large bowl that was my life and voila!
They should've taken me to a meeting that very same day I picked up a drink.
You see, booze changed me in the beginning, it seemed to me.
All those feelings just seemed to go away.

Those less—than feelings.

As a matter of fact, through the years of drinking I just didn't even care.

As long as I had that drink.

But by the time I came into a recovery program, I couldn't stop drinking

and all those feeling of less than were back big time.

The only difference at that point was most of the comments about not being good enough were coming from inside my own head.

Having had drunk most of my feelings away only to have them back twice as bad.

Now I'm in a program of change.

Working the what they call the steps in all my affairs.

Really looking at all those dark spots that make me—well, me.

Good, bad, or indifferent.

Uncovering those less—than feelings.

Learning to own what is truly mine and what isn't.

Knowing that I'm not all that bad, that there is some good.

Learning to live with the fact that I'm okay without a using today.

That by working with my sponsor,

doing the steps, and taking life one moment at a time, It will be ok.

So that's that.

Oh, and before I forget to tell you just what kind of card carrying member I am,

ask yourself,

"Am I one?"

A card-carrying member of

The Less—Than Club . . . .

Freedom to be Me

For once in my life I would like to be free.

Free to make decisions that are good for me.

But that wasn't always how it was.

Once I found alcohol, the ability to make choices and sane decision-making were gone.

Alcoholic thinking was what I would do.

Most of my life I was like a great chess player in my mind.

Always two or three steps ahead, moving the pieces on the board for the outcome I wanted.

Manipulating the people around me, if I could.

To produce the final victory, which was the drink or drug in my hand.

But there was no real freedom in my thinking at that time in my life.

Old John Barleycorn was making the real moves on my chessboard life.

Leading me into thinking that I was the one making these great choices and leading me down the road of what I thought was happiness.

But there was no real happiness by the end of my using.

Nor was there any real freedom from my thinking.

The insanity of this disease was keeping me out there using when the end was well over. What I didn't know was Old John had moved all my pieces on the board into no freedom for me.

Now I'm in the program, working on these steps.

Having put down that drink and drug was one of the hardest decisions to make. Especially when my thinking was so messed up that at sometimes in that first year, drinking sounded right.

The alcohol thinking and the insane decisions were still right there.

I thank God for the old-timers that helped me out.

Showing me away from the insane life I was living.

Helping me understand that even if I wanted to drink,
I didn't have to.

This was for me my first real freedom.

Knowing that I had choices again.

But what if I chose wrong?

Well that's what a sponsor is for—to ask.

That's what the twelve steps are for—to do.

Having cleared away the old chessboard and getting honest with me.

Not drinking or drugging was but the first of many decisions that I would make.

Learning how to live one day and sometimes one moment means to make choices and decisions for myself.

Wrong or right I've learned how to do this.

With the help of a higher power, a sponsor, having a home group and being part of a Fellowship.

Not just a side line watcher. But a doer.

Jumping in with both feet as they say.

Talking to other people in the Fellowship.

Letting others know where I am and learning to have people help me when my thinking isn't great.

It's not so much the drink or drug today, it's my thinking, my decision making.

The choices that can put me in the wrong place so fast that I feel I'm back at square one. But the ability to make right choices for me is the best freedom of all.

Being able to think clearly because there is no alcohol or drugs in me is one of the greatest feelings to date.

Right or wrong, the choices we make and being accountable for our actions is freedom of self.

But the best thing of all is that I can be me.

That I am free,

and the Freedom to be Me . . . .

Responsible

Just think, when people say things like,
"I'm responsible."
Are they saying that they're owning up to something?
Or just responsible for someone or both?
When I hear things throughout the day,
I'm reminded of the fact that I'm on my second life.
Not only am I living today—but also my life is so much better because
I try to be more responsible in my entire affairs today.
Talk about an open book—geez.
My friends are not the same as when I came into recovery.
Not that that mattered much.
Most were gone due to me and my drinking by then anyway.
Now I can't say that everyone I've met in sobriety I liked right off the
bat.
Heck, deep down I didn't even like myself.
Some just didn't like me and some I just didn't get along with.
An old timer once told me,
"You can love them all, just some of them you can love the least."
But for the most part I've tried to keep it simple.
My sponsor would tell me, "Pray—Pray—Pray a lot.
Then do some more praying."
When someone looks like they need help or a simple handshake, that's
me giving
"It away."
When people ask me today,
"What are you doing?"

I can tell them and not feel uncomfortable about what, "They think."
Like most, this is hard for me.
Hard in the sense because I would like people to like me.
But I know deep down that that takes time.
So guess what?
I pray.
So when people say,
"I'm responsible."
I know I am sometimes.
I'm responsible for my own sobriety today.
My happiness, even my own sadness.
People can be happy or sad.
Mad or glad.
Irate or joyous beyond belief.
And here it is—it's none of my business.
When I start trusting in my higher power—fully trust, life is good.
When I take the time out to help someone and most of all myself today,
I'm a little bit more, Responsible . . . .

I thought I Knew

Long ago before I even came into a recovery program,
I thought that my life was somewhat okay.
Way before I had that first drink.
There were times that I did know some things.
I knew how to do the simple things.
Like eat, get dressed and even tie my own shoes.
But most of these I had to learn.
Being shown by my parents or my older brothers.
As I grew a little bit older, I started doing these things on my own.
But there were other things that I slowly started to pick up.
Like the habit of lying.
Playing one parent against one another.
The fine art of getting what I wanted, when I wanted.
All these behaviors that I thought were very individual, just to me.
Time passed—I found alcohol—that should've been the end of the story.
But it wasn't.
Just the beginning of more things that I would pick up along the way of my using.
More time passed—I had had enough.
Enough of living in the way that I was.
The lying, cheating and manipulating people to get what I needed.
It just didn't work anymore by the end.
Coming into a program of recovery and still holding on to some, if not most of my
so-called individual habits.

Being mad that it was over.
Feeling relief in hearing that I was not alone.
Learning that I didn't know—but that I could learn.
Going from the, "Ya buts." To the, "I know." Back to, "Ya but if."
To later saying, "I didn't know."
Hearing that there was hope.
Learning a new way of living and being willing to change.
Picking up new things to help me stay sober and happy.
To clean house.
Letting go.
A higher power.
How not to drink one day at time and being okay with me today.
Laughing at myself.
Time passed some more—Today, right now. I can look back in light of
this and laugh at the things I would say to my sponsor like,
"If you only knew?"
My sponsor would look at me and shake his head,
'til I'd stop and say,
"I thought I Knew."

Tune In & Tune Out

It has been quite some time since I've actually tuned out something—about an hour after I woke up this morning to be exact.
It's the tuning in that I have to work on a daily basis to do.
Tuning out has always been easy to me.
As long as I can remember there were times I'd tune things out.
People, places and even things.
What's that saying?
"Out of sight, out of mind."
I used to love that one.
When I was young and working outside a lot we used to say,
"Looks good from my house."
Even when we worked in another state at the time.
Places and people were easy too.
Tuning out where I've been when I have made a mess of things.
If I couldn't get what I wanted—well, I'd move on.
Tuning out the,
Where you been, or
catch up to you soon,
and let's not forget the, I'll be there.
That one always worked.
And things—there were always things to tune out.
Many things by the time I stopped using.
Now it's to the tuning in on a daily basis.
It's really the same thing just in reverse.
But boy do I have a hard time sometimes!
But thanks to recovery,

the program, the writings and my friends, tuning in has been a little better.

Not perfect by any means, but thank God,

I don't have to live up to other people's aspects of what, "They think."

Working on cleaning up the messes that I made when using.

Cleaning house as recovery says.

Owning what's mine, learning what isn't.

Tuning in to what's going on around me at any moment.

When it comes to places—tuning in was just showing up—on time too—that one was some work.

Still is, if I'm not careful.

Working on things like—putting in a full day at work,

not thinking that they owe me.

Having respect for one's home.

No longer looking through their medicine cabinet

or helping to look for their wallet when it was in my own pocket at the time.

Willing to work on making amends with the people I've hurt.

Tuning in to the feelings that made me start down that road of resentments.

And tuning out the negative behaviors that I would do.

Taking the time to tune in to other people's needs, not my own.

Today—Tuning in means a lot more to me in many ways.

Not being too far ahead of myself.

Taking the time to see what's going on in my life.

Good or bad.

Letting recovery help me to learn how to be happy right where I'm supposed to be at this time,

right here, right now.

Tuning in to the higher power that I can understand.

And just letting, "It" happen.

Staying grateful.

But most important to just,

Tune In & Tune Out . . . .

First

First—Just sitting here now and writing that one word out was one.
First—Just writing that again was one.
First—Ok, I think you got what I mean.
At least I think you do.
But there are many firsts that we go through in just one day.
Sometimes even in one moment at a time there are firsts.
As far back as I can remember, they were there.
Those moments where I experienced doing something for the very first time in my life.
If my mother were alive she might have said the first time I kicked or the first time I cried.
When I walked or when I ran.
First A from all the D s.
But as I write this down there was one first that and I hope and pray to my higher power that I don't forget.
Is when my mother was standing at the door and welcoming me back in from the hell that was my life from using once again.
Stepping through that door was the first time that I had had enough.
Enough of the way I was living.
Enough of the way that drinking had run my life.
The first time I looked into her eyes and cried no more—just no more.
God willing,
there have been many and God willing,
there are still a lot to come.
That first time I saw that meeting book.

That first deep down feeling of shame and anger when I was walking to that side door at that Church.
That first time that I can remember seeing so many shoelaces.
Where an hour seemed like days.
By the grace of a power greater than I there were many firsts. And do you know what?
I hope to my higher power that I still have many more.
For without the firsts in my life,
there would be no life at all.
I need to always remember—just for today,
that I'm powerless against alcohol and that my life had become unmanageable.
That today is the first day of the rest of my life.
I've heard it in recovery that life happens regardless if I show up or not.
I choose to show up sober and clean so that I can have one more first among many today. Just one more first,
like they say—First things First . . . .

Where did I park My Life

Why does it always seem like when I have it all ironed out in my life, something always comes along to remind me that the only certain in life is change?
I mean really,
just what more does my higher power have in store for me in this life?
My sponsor would probably say, "Anything and everything."
He's like that, very vague—when I'm looking for a direct answer in my life.
Now don't get me wrong, in the beginning there was a lot that I needed help with. Help with the simple fact that I couldn't drink in safety any longer.
Help with not knowing where to turn.
Help with the fact that, at times, it felt like my life was over.
In the beginning it seemed that drinking wasn't the problem.
It was my parents, my bosses, or whomever I was with at the time.
As simple as that.
But what I didn't know at the time was that I had given alcohol free reign of my life.
It told me that I knew more than my parents at the ripe old age of 14.
Wherever I worked my bosses would tell me,
"This is how it's done."
I would say,
"But I know a better way."
The same with any relationships that I was in at the time, I would say,
"Do what I say, not what I do."
Ya, like that worked.

But alcohol told me that I was right, and they were wrong.
Did you ever wonder why WAR was sometimes spelled in capital letters?
I think for me it stands for We Are Right.
So does that mean You Are Wrong?
Mr. Webster's definition of YAW is a verb.
The definition of the word is,
"To deviate from the intended course. To move unsteadily."
Could the problem really be me?
Alcohol said, "It was ok."
But it was anything but ok.
All this time fighting the WAR on others,
when the truth of the matter was the YAW, right in my face.
Looking right back at me with blood shot eyes,
un-brushed teeth and no clean socks.
How unsteadily I moved through life.
How deviated from my intended course did I go.
And still, alcohol said, "It was ok."
I don't think that there was ever a time in my life that I said,
"Gee, I think I'd like to be an alcoholic
and that I would like my life to be unmanageable."
It just happened.
That's the truth of the matter.
Neither right nor wrong, but the truth.
There's still a lot of work ahead for me.
But with the help from people.
From meetings and a higher power to help me on this intended course of sobriety.
To move somewhat steadily through this life,
to know that today, that the only certainty is change
and to stop living in the past where I would wonder,
"Where did I park My Life?" . . . .

Signposts

A lot has happened since I started to go to a recovery program.
A lot of choices too, hard choices sometimes—sometimes not.
Looking back at myself, cleaning one's house, as they say.
Doing what people said to do,
if I wanted what they had.
Looking for those signposts that would help me along the way of recovery
and those that would lead me back out.
There was a time when most—if not all—of my individual signposts I just didn't see,
or wouldn't.
When I finally stopped running,
When I honestly looked back.
To see that there were times where one should've stopped.
Stopped what I was doing at that time.
Going from job to job—because my using was more important at the time.
Leaving school too early was one.
But ya couldn't tell me then.
Making sure I made enough to pay my dealer on payday,
only to have them front me some more that same day.
Telling my relationships, parents, even my employer,
"That I'll make it up with them next week."
But next week never seemed to come.
Working and planning my next drink or drug seemed like the right plan to do.

I would start on Tuesday writing down how much I needed by Friday to
pay rent,
car payment, insurance and my dealer.
It looked so good on paper 'til it would hit me that I was late on most
of my other responsibilities—never counting in things like phone,
gas, water and lights.
God, then there was food.
Didn't alcohol have vitamins?
Well there's one down I didn't have to worry about.
So my list that started on Tuesday—by Wednesday it looked different.
I would put in some overtime,
what would it take to catch up?
"I would pay rent right off the bat." I'll say.
Car payment next and dealer.
Put some money on the gas and lights.
Did I really need a phone?
By Thursday my list had shortened somehow.
"Okay, this is what I'll do—rent, dealer, bar tab." I'd say.
I can't believe I forgot that one.
Car payment, gas and lights.
It all looked so good on paper.
"This is what I should do when I get paid tomorrow." I said to myself.
God, its Friday. I made it through another week.
Going to the bank with my list in hand.
Getting my money and heading to the bar to meet some friends.
Asking for a drink and being refused until I paid off my tab.
Giving over what I owed to my dealer and asking for more.
"Sure, you're good for it." He'd say.
Heading back to the bar to get my thoughts in place.
Meeting up with people that were doing the same thing as I was at that
moment.
Not getting home until well after dark.
Where was my list?
Let's go to that party they're having.
Coming to sometime on Sunday.
How the heck did I miss a day?
Where was all my money?
Somebody took it, I just know it!

Where am I?

And where are my shoes?

Finding my way back home just to clean up to go to bed.

By Monday morning, looking at my refection in the mirror,

telling myself, "That I did it again."

"What happened?" I'd ask myself.

Feeling all those crappie thoughts again.

Having to bum smokes off of my co-workers and going right to bed when I got home.

So by Tuesday I would start out making my list, "This is what I will do."

I said to myself.

There were many signposts along the way—some I just didn't see.

It all looked so great on paper.

"I can do this, if I just follow my list." I'd say.

My list of Signposts . . . .

Time, God, & Recovery.

Not too long ago someone asked me to help him in the program of recovery.
"What kind of help?" I asked him,
Looking down at the ground, he said,
"I don't know.
It's like I can't stop and I need help."
As he looked up at me again I said,
"It's okay—neither could I in the beginning."
"In time," I said, "Things change."
"With God's help there is release,
and within recovery, there I found hope."
"Time?" he asked.
"Ya—One of the big ones." I said to him.
"Time to sober up,
time to heal."
"What about God?" He asked.
"What about God?" I shot right back.
"I don't believe in God."
He told me—as he looked down at his shoes.
Asking him to look at me, I told him,
"Ya—but He believes in you."
"Then there's recovery." I said.
"That this is the place where I've found hope.
In these meeting I've been taught how to live one day at a time."
Are you still asking me for help?" I said to him.
"I think so?" Was his reply.

"But I don't know where to start?"
Looking at him and seeing me staring back, I said,
"If you want what we have,
the doors of recovery are always open,
so come on in.
There you'll find a new way of life in
Time, God, & Recovery."

House on Blue Lawn

It's been some time now without my friend.
It's been too long that I helped him out of bed.
When I close my eyes, and think of the times we had.
Just hanging around, and not really doing much.

It's been quite some time, and I can still hear
The grinding of his teeth.
Or the touch of his hair when he would take my hand,
and help him rub his head.

There is no marker for my friend.
No land to stand on,
and place something in.

There is a place where he rests though.
Where once he grew up,
and came back in the end.

When I close my eyes,
and then look out onto the lake.
I know my friend is with me,
today,
and until the end.

It's been some time now.
No marker to say,

that my friend was even here.
But I know when I see the lake,
that my friend is everywhere.

So I kneel down by the lakeside,
and pray all alone.
Placing flowers in the water,
in front of his home.

Now I sit, and I pray,
in the early hours of dawn.
While listening to the loons on the lake,
in the House on Blue Lawn . . . .

When Life
&
Reality Collide

Preface

Starting out writing this preface I couldn't help going back into my head just to get my thoughts in order—my own room six.

The many people who helped me get this far and they're a lot.

The teachers that helped me understand that there are many writing styles.

The help from the publishers online chat—at 2 am.

To a woman that is probably the most unselfish person I've met since my mother passed away. She helped me look at my writing, changed what needed to be changed and still kept it me. Thank you, Laura.

To my friends in recovery—good and bad.

I'm still learning to play well with others.

Looking at these stories taking shape was a reality.

Seeing those around us and ourselves change for the better—most of the time—that is life.

Having those thoughts go into action—to seeing where my life and my reality come together.

"It's God's will." They keep telling me.

I'm just along for the ride, unless I take my will back.

Hey, I'm still trying to play well with others here.

Most of us have our concept of reality and where our life is at.

Fancied or real, when they do come together it can be some of the best moments in our lives—or the worst, it seems.

One of the quotes my Mom used to preach is,

"There's right, there's wrong, and there's the truth; and the truth is neither or; it just is."

But my friends tell me, "You better hold on to your seat, you're in for one hell of a ride when they do collide" . . .

Be Where I Am—Today

When the time came and the drink just wasn't doing it for me anymore, I stopped.

But it didn't happen just like that, nor was it easy.

There were circumstances, many circumstances.

Just because there was that day—when all my chips were on the table—the cards were out.

All the bluffing and conning was done.

The truth was written all over my face as I looked in the mirror.

All the drinking that I had done over that last couple of days just wasn't working anymore.

Starting out young and thinking that the world owed me something when I was drinking most of the time lead me down that long road of disappointments.

To not wanting to be where I was at that time in the end.

Drinking just to fit into the surroundings that were there at the time.

Feeling the—not part of thoughts.

Drinking when I thought it was cool with my friends.

Being consumed with thinking of drinking every day.

Trying to make the changes on my own and not succeeding so many times that the drink seemed like the only thing to do—at that moment.

Stepping into the wrong places so many times that it seemed that that's what I was placed here on this world to do—make mistakes.

Never once thinking that the drink in my hand or the places where my drinking had taken me was the problem.

When I started out thinking—just a few—the few that would end up in some other state of mind or place—if you drank like me.

There was no such thing as one.

Coming to and thinking, "I've done it again."

Asking myself—no yelling at myself—"Why can't I get a break."

While I would search the sofa for lost change for that bottle down the street.

A lot has changed in my life since coming to a program on recovery.

One—I don't drink today—no matter what.

Two—I've come to believe in something greater than myself and thank God not the bottle.

Three—That the road I am on has already been paved by those who came before me as long as I'm willing to ask for help.

Staying away from that first drinking—to seeing what happens to those of us who just can't let go.

Being aware of my surroundings—and being content right at this moment in time—are huge things.

Things that we all can do with some time.

It's not the destination but the journey that I should be enjoying.

Being happy my life has changed.

But most important for me is to Be Where I Am—Today . . .

Side Door

Once in a while I still hear that phrase in meetings, "This is the last house on the street."

For some of us have found that the program of recovery works as long as we work at it and stay around 'til the miracle happens.

Some of us have been sent by the courts, while others by their employers.

Even some by just the looks on the faces of family, friends or even their children.

Still others find that it was over for them and came in on their own.

For most of us it started from a side walk to that side door.

Some use the front, but the first meeting I attended was going through that side door, to the last house on the block.

Walking up the side path of that building felt like the longest walk I had ever taken.

Feeling all those emotions all at once was like sharp little stingers hitting me all over.

Like a bite of a winter's day.

Feeling glad that it was over—no more hiding—no more broken promises.

Just no more.

Feeling hopeless and tired, but most of all as I walked closer to that side door, I felt mad, pissed really.

This is where my life had taken me, I thought.

Some piece of work I turned out to be.

It's not like I woke one morning and said, "Gee, let's be a drunk today; that looks like fun."

As fun as standing on hot coals to see how long they took to burn through the soles of my shoes.

Yah, that would be fun.

"But my best thinking got me here." I've been told.

That's me all right.

Thinking I've done right so far—right.

Putting the "Fun" back into dysfunctional.

Oh, for cry eye! All this and I haven't even opened that darn door yet.

When I finally do and the first person I see says, "Hi. How you doing?"

I looked up real quick and say, "Fine—couldn't be better! Just call me Mr. Fun Bags!"

As I walked right by them to the back of the hall, standing there with my arms crossed and passing judgment.

Thank God for the folks that put up with me in the beginning.

All that whining they had to endure and all they kept saying is, "Don't drink, no matter what."

As time passed many things have changed. That long walk isn't as long anymore.

Mostly due to the fact that I don't drink today—just today.

Sometimes I'm even the one at the door now saying, "Come in. Welcome." To that person coming in the door.

Looking at the face of me mirroring right back at me so many years ago. As they come through that Side Door . . .

Re—Accept

Accepting the things I cannot change—how many times have I heard that one. A lot.
But that's okay.
Accepting and moving on is one of the things a person does in life.
In or out of the halls of recovery.
Looking back now I see there were some things I had to accept—right there on the spot.
The admitting that I was powerless was the first step in the right direction—it was the accepting part of it all. Well, it didn't happen overnight.
But it did happen.
Sometimes quickly, sometimes not.
There are so many layers of myself to accept; just add infinity.
But it does happen and you know what?
The ones that came quickly were most of the ones I had to go back and re-accept.
Learning that I was powerless over everything—not just my drinking.
Alcohol just didn't pick and choose what it was going to ruin in my life.
It didn't sit on some bench in the park saying, "See that guy over there? I'm going to take his wife away today, and see that girl there? She's going to lose her kids by the end of the week.
Oh, and see that young couple sitting on the grass? Guess which one I'm going to take out when they drive home tonight."
For me it was everything.
I gave alcohol and drugs free rein over my life.

So really it never took—I gave—just to have more.

Which is my favorite one anyway. More.

Re-accepting that I'm an alcoholic was just the swinging of the fence gate and seeing that there was a path to walk down.

Having to admit that my life was unmanageable came in time.

God, don't 'cha just love that one—time.

Things I must endure.

Myself—I like to look at it as—things I might enjoy.

Considering that the joy is in the journey.

When I stopped sitting at the buffet table of insanity and stopped shoveling it in—looking for more—things started to change.

As long as I stayed willing, open, and honest.

The re-accepting on a daily basis hasn't been that bad.

As long as I stayed away from that buffet table.

As I stay sober and started my journey down that path through the gate many years ago I've heard a lot of the "How to's" or "What not to do's."

But the very things that help me the most is a belief in something greater than myself and to know it.

Not just in my head but the truth of what I am. In my heart.

They say the longest or hardest distance is that space between the head and the heart.

So I ask for help today.

Like I did yesterday, and God willing, I will ask again tomorrow.

The path that I'm on can be flat or rocky, shady or sunny, and sometimes I can see down that path for quite a distance.

Other times it takes a sharp bend and I have to hold on.

Either way I still have to come to terms with something about myself or others.

To acknowledge a fact or truth and come to terms with it.

Every day I have to Re—Accept . . .

Foundations

In going to meetings now for quite some time I've heard throughout the years on the "How" of the program—honesty, openness, and willingness.

Three of the cornerstones of sobriety.

But in the beginning the ground was anything but solid—still very shaky due to the drinking and drugging that I did.

Just because I stopped using didn't mean the ground on which I stood was solid.

It took time.

One of the ingredients in my foundation—time.

People that came before me told me things straight up.

Like, "Keep it simple." "Keep coming." and "Don't drink."

There was no way that I could even think about building any kind of house on the foundation that I thought I had.

One that was built on using.

The lying—stealing.

The not knowing what I didn't know when I was out there.

So what makes a good foundation?

One that can stand up in time.

Who can say—I think that it varies with who you are, who you talk to.

What their life has been and what they're doing in their life at that moment.

But in sobriety and a program of change, my foundations are in my experiences.

In my younger years I worked with a small family mason company.

Starting off as a laborer to a brick layer. Hard work but good pay.

One of the things that was shown to me by the old man who owned the company was the first step in any building was the foundation.

How it was set in the ground, if it was level.

Looking it over with just his eyes. Cleaning off the top to start laying bricks down.

I should've known I had a problem even back then when I was told to make the mortar for the crew. How mad I was to think I wasn't going to be a brick layer on my second day. He brought me to the side of the building where there was a big pile of sand along with a machine to make the mortar.

Next to that was a pallet full of small bags of mortar mix.

He then started to show me how to prepare the mix.

Starting with water, and then throwing in the power mix with some sand.

Slowly having the machine turn the mixture 'til it was just the right consistency to lay the brick on.

Not too dry, not too wet.

When he first showed me I thought is this guy for real, how hard was it to do.

Well, I found out. It took time.

Especially when you have the crew yelling down from the staging waiting for their mortar so they can lay more bricks down.

But I learned. Never really admitting that the old man was right.

Heck. He knew—he just looked down at me and shook his head, and told me to keep trying. You'll get it.

Just because I showed up for my second day didn't mean I knew what I was doing.

Even how to make what I thought was the simplest thing in the world, like mortar.

Same as when I came to the program—I just didn't know the "How" yet.

I had to learn to listen, and then listen to learn.

You don't know—if you don't know—and I definitely didn't know, but I learned.

Same with this program. I learned and am still learning even today.

Learning that the foundations are in the program—just ask to be shown.

The ones that came before me have shown me when I was ready to change and start building my new life.

They helped me with the fact that the hole that I had dug for myself could turn into the base for the rest of my life—in my new Foundations . . .

Unteachable

There I was standing behind my friend—helping him clean up at the sink in our home.

Leaning over him cleaning my hands with the hot water running from the faucet, when he started to reach out with one of his hands.

Stopping him with the concern that he would burn himself with the hot water—he started reaching out with his other hand as I placed the first one back onto the sink.

"What are you doing?" I said to him. "Stop messing around. You'll get burnt with this water. It's hot." I told him again.

You see, when I met this young man he was living in a group home.

A home provided by the state that helped him with his disabilities.

His so-called maladjustments to life.

His body may not have been sharp, but let me be the first to tell you that that's where it stopped.

He was bright all right, bright in the sense that he knew what he wanted and how to get it.

That's for sure.

The young man that I was taking care of was nonverbal—meaning—and for lack of any better words—he was unable to speak in any traditional way.

But let me say this right off the bat, he spoke in volumes.

With signs that were modified by him that he knew. It was up to us to learn and interpret what he was asking or wanting.

Oh, sure, he knew how to say please and thank you. Drink or more. One of his favorites was the sign for milk—lots of milk.

You knew if he was happy and believe me—you knew if he wasn't.

He knew how to write phonetically on a Qwerty board. He would spell out things that he wanted or needed or just to say hi.

He even asked for his room to be painted red—all red. But that's a story for another time.

When I met him a few years before he lived with me, the people that ran the group home told me he was unteachable.

That he had learned all that they were able to give. That he had reached his potential in his learning with his disability.

I think of today in my recovery—had they told me that I was unteachable.

That I couldn't—for whatever reason—that that was it.

That you're hopeless to learn how to stay sober and clean.

Sorry we can't help you, thanks for coming.

But they didn't—they said, "Just keep coming back; it gets better."

They were right.

Looking back now and seeing with somewhat of a clear mind. There were teachers all around me or better yet—and I love this—agents of God, as I call them.

People that came into my life to show me things, anything really.

From my parents to my brothers to my school teachers of my youth.

To my heroes of life. The cowboys and firefighters to the astronauts that I would look up into the night sky dreaming on flying to the moon with them.

To my favorite comic book writer. To the people that would show me how to do the things to live a happy and useful life.

Then there were the ones that showed me the road or the door on using—by their own actions this was shown. How to get it and where.

And there came a time that I did it all on my own. Just think—no more teachers, I thought.

Learning all I needed to know for my life seemed right back then.

Heedless of where my drinking or what my behavior was doing to me. But no one showed me the end.

Oh, I've seen people get sick or even pass away. But that wasn't me.

The denial of this disease is wider than any ocean I've seen.

But when the end comes—as it surely does with us—there are some lessons that can't be taught—they have to be lived, or we die.

Now I have new teachers.

Ones that have done the things that help me on this road of life.

The changes—the up's and down's—showing me by example what to do on a daily basis to live happy, joyous, and free.

Teaching me the ropes, as they say, on cleaning up my life—and there have been many.

Thank God for that too. I just stopped looking or thinking I needed them.

But they were there.

Being open and willing was just the beginning to this journey that has many ways to live a happy life.

I really only have two types of teachers today.

Those that show me what to do and those that show me what not to do.

Being teachable, willing to learn new things about myself. Staying in the now.

And there I was standing behind my friend.

Helping him clean up in the bathroom of our home. Thinking he was the one I was showing what to do when that God moment struck.

I stepped back and said, "What is it you want to do?"

He slowly reached out and started to turn the faucet on. Taking my hand into his to feel the temperature of the water—not too hot—not too cold. Just right.

Seeing him slowly reaching for the soap by the side of the sink and it hit me like a freight train.

"Do you want to wash your hands?" I asked.

With a big smile and a sign that said yes. We washed our hands together.

I had stopped being the teacher and was being taught.

They say, "When you're ready, the teacher will appear."

Here was someone that when meeting them for the first time they said he was unteachable.

One only has to be open and willing to see that the only one teachable was me.

That I just had to let it happen—being open to learn from the Unteachable . . .

The Other One Too

There I was not knowing that I had done it right or not.
Running through the living room and into the kitchen.
Stopping there in front of my mom.
She was so happy when she looked down at me.
The kitchen smelled of dough and cinnamon.
She stopped what she was doing, I think she was baking. Because she reached over the stove and gave me a cookie.
"You have made me real proud." She said leaning over to give me a kiss on the forehead.
"Mom. Shh." I said with my hands on my hips. "I'm not a child you know."
She just smiled at me and said, "I know my small grown man."
I walked to the window and saw that my Dad was cutting the grass and it made me feel all excited again.
Running out the kitchen through the back hall and out through the side door, I sprang.
"Dad, Dad!" I yelled over the sound of the lawn mower.
But he couldn't hear me.
Is he gonna' see me? I thought. Dad always said never play or run around when he's doing the lawn. But I just had to show him.
"Dad, Dad!" I yelled again.
Just then my father was turning a corner with the lawn mower. When he saw me he waved.
"Dad!" I yelled again.

As my father turned around with the lawnmower and was coming towards me, he must have seen how excited I was and stopped the machine.

"What is it son?" He asked as he walked up the side of the walkway brushing grass off his pants.

He stopped in front of me wiping the sweat off his forehead with a handkerchief he took out of his pocket and looked down at me.

Is he gonna' see? I was so happy.

"Dad, look, look!"

My father must have thought that I had gone mad. There I was jumping up and down screaming, "Look, Look!"

"Look at what son?" My father asked, looking at me and over to our house.

"Is everything okay?"

"Has something happened to your mother?" He asked, looking past me again.

"No, no Dad, look at me."

My father stopped and looked at me. He looked me up and down.

He had to see, he just had to. I was so proud.

"Well son." He said. "Just what am I looking at here?"

As I looked up at him and said, "Mom says she's so proud of me."

As the words came out in a rush of air.

"She even gave me a cookie." I said. As I tried to breathe in just as the words were flowing out of me.

"Well, only one, but it was close to dinner time." I told him.

With my hands down at my side, my head held high. I put one foot out so my Dad could see.

"Well, son, that is something." He said as he put his handkerchief away.

"Your Mom's right, that is something to be very proud of. Very proud indeed." He said.

This is great I thought to myself, when my mom saw, she gave me a treat.

Just think what my father would give me.

My thoughts were everywhere.

"Son, I'll tell you what I'll do for you." He said.

This is it, maybe he'll give me some money so I can buy some candy down at the corner store or maybe?

"Son, since you're so grown up now." He said with a smile on his face.

"I'll tell you what." He added.

Here it comes I thought, closing my eyes and putting my hand out for my Dad.

"You can help with the rest of the lawn." He said.

As he turned and walked away I could hear him say.

"Great job on tying your shoe.

But before you help me make sure you do The Other One Too." . . .

Why

How often we, as people—as a country full of different cultures, different diversities—look at one another—differently.

One would think that someone with disabilities has a hard time understanding or comprehending what is going on around them in their everyday life.

On September 11, 2001, as with most people around the country, my day started off like the one before.

I woke up, had something to eat and went to work.

I have been given the opportunity to work with people with disabilities for over 10 years now and was at a job site with individuals that have some form of handicaps.

People that don't know this type of field often say to me that I must have a lot of patience and I usually tell them yes they do, for putting up with me.

As the morning went on there were reports of a plane that had just collided with one of the world trade centers in New York City.

As the clients and I walked down the hallway we started to hear more.

Now a second plane had hit and more people were gone.

I decided then to bring all of them back to their office where we could find out what was really going on.

Like most companies word spread quickly, but this was different. You could feel it in the air.

Small groups of people were gathering.

Talking about what was going on.

You could not escape it—it was everywhere.

By this time we had heard of what had happened in DC and still we didn't know why.

By break time the company we were at had placed a television out in the cafeteria where even more people gathered as we silently watched—as two mighty buildings came down. I was very honest with them at this time, how could I not be—it was everywhere.

I gave them the choice of having lunch in their office that day or if they wanted to they could eat in the café where they usually sat.

Explaining to them that there was a T.V. on and many people of many diversities were gathering.

Some of them went—while some chose to stay in their office.

There were ones that wanted to go home. Didn't really blame them. I called my family as soon as I had a chance, just to make sure that they were all right.

As our workday came to a close, we all talked and discussed about what had happened to our country this day.

Here now are just some of the things that were said by someone who on first glance one might think that they really didn't understand what's going on around them.

"It's an awful thing—these people died doing nothing wrong."

"That plane and things—that hurts and it makes me sad inside."

"I'm sad for the people that are no longer here and for their families, scary."

"Lots of people died today, but lots of people were able to get out of some of the buildings. This we should be happy about—it is a sad day."

"It's a very sad thing that happened and I don't know why we have to live like this. I guess that's the b-side of life."

As tears slowly formed in my eyes, we all sat in silence.

Remembering what had happened this day in New York City, DC, and Pennsylvania.

No difference.

No wall of misunderstanding.

No handicaps.

Just people.

I came away with the same feelings that the clients had.

Feeling very sad and scared and the unending question that we all felt that day.

"Why?" . . .

Apples and Ostriches

It's as plan as that—these two completely different things—it seems I'm completely drawn to.

I mean really—when I first heard the saying, "The apple didn't fall far from the tree." I thought that they were giving me a compliment as I was bringing the pitcher of beer over to the table that Dad and I were sitting at. Not even looking for trouble when my Dad told the guys around the bar—"Here he is, boys—just like me, the old man."

Feeling embarrassed on being put on the spot—hiding my head—better yet, my feelings.

So they don't think less of me.

When I know even then that I was no mere drinker.

Something about wanting more than what was on the table.

Isn't that why I got up to fetch the beer in the first place.

Feeling less than the people I was with always made me run from confrontation—any confrontations, even when I was with—oh, I don't know—say, everybody.

When someone said something I didn't like or disagreed with—I would turn away or hide my head.

There were only a few times I'd speak up, for the most part I hid my head like that ostrich. Hoping that it would just go away.

When I start ignoring the things I have to do—placing my head in the sand or taking someone else's inventory, pointing out their apple. Life seems so much harder.

Half measures—hell, I wasn't doing even that.

When I was drinking a lot of things didn't happen due to me hiding my head or just looking the other way.

Keep low as I would put it. Not sticking my head out there.

Why draw attention to me and my using. Heck, I know how bad I was—well some, I didn't need you to tell me.

Years later I'm in recovery, and left to my own I can still hide my head in the sand—not taking chances or putting myself out there for change. Even to look at all of me, good or bad.

The things that stand out most about these two are that I'm just like them in certain circumstances.

In the program we hear about the apple on our heads—or don't put your head in the sand. Like the ostrich I can—at times—not look at myself.

Not having that faith at times to walk through what life has given me at that moment and that's just it, it's a moment.

A moment that will pass.

Avoiding it doesn't help or make it go away. It's what I used to do.

Hide, run.

"Just someone make it go away." I'd say.

The farther I stuck my head in the sand—the more the problem seemed to get big. 'Til I take my head out and look—really look at the situation or problem.

Learning to have faith, when there is none.

It's not going away when I put my hands up to my face to cover my eyes saying la la la. It's not happening, it's not happening.

I've spent too much time wasted in my using past doing this.

But here in the Fellowship I've learned that we don't have to hide our heads in the sand—like that ostrich.

Then there's the apple.

The one I can see on everybody else's head but mine.

You can see mine—I can see yours, kind of weird don't'cha think?

But it's there nevertheless.

That apple.

I'd like to think that my apple is nice and shiny, full of life. But just looking back at my life, at a young age—heck, even as I'm writing this down now the apple didn't fall far from the tree.

I don't have to be carrying a pitcher of beer back to the table to start looking at others wrongly. Picking them apart just so I could feel better. Hell, the time I get back to really looking at myself my apple is pointed out by my friends that it's grown into an orchard.

See how, "They live, not living to let live." To the point of things in my life just start slipping away from me.

I've been shown that there is the Program and the Fellowship. Two very different things.

The more I stick around the more I hear, "Live in the solution and not the problem."

"Learn to live with it or let it go." Oh, and one of my favorites.

"Do you want to be happy or do you want to be right."

With the help of the program I can take care of my apple and learn to leave others alone.

The same can be said for the fellowship, where this is the place I can learn that I don't have to hide my head in the sand.

Take some action, either doing the next right thing, having healthier boundaries, cleaning up the wreckage of my past with those creditors.

Life's going to happen regardless if I have my head in the sand or looking at others and not staying on my side of the street.

All I can do is really just work on me and keep a look out for those hiccups on this road of changes I'd like to call Apples and Ostriches . . .

Room Six

I've heard the suggestions like change your playground, stay away from those old haunts. Stay out of your own head. To hearing that popping sound as I take my head out of my—well, you know where.

Sitting down with a friend one day having coffee. Talking about how we felt and joking about the times we put those, "For rent signs," in our minds.

Thinking that this great machine I like to call my brain will fix the problem sometimes. And we laughed—knowing that we share the same way of thinking.

We started telling each other how it is when we go to that place in our heads that I like to call room six.

Room six—just the name sounds amusing when I say it out loud.

But it's not. Just one room. My room, your own room.

We all have a place that we go to when things are going on in our life.

Room six is a large room with one window and peeling ceiling paint with wallpaper walls.

Well, at least what's left of the wallpaper, that is.

Looks like the preceding leaseholder had some fun tearing some of the wallpaper off in three of the corners.

But why just three? Now there's a query.

Least they had their hands free.

Or maybe not.

It could've been done with their teeth I reason to myself. I've even heard that one could use their own toes to pick away at themselves to the point of bleeding.

But let's not go there at the moment.

Needless to say I don't have my hands free along with the taste of wallpaper that doesn't appeal to me either.

I haven't been in room six long enough to think about it and there's that word right in itself—think.

That's why I'm in room six now, anyway, is it not?

My large room has but one chair, tanned in color and by the window.

Listen to me, my oversized room, ha!

The chair is old and worn with age. Looks like somebody sat in it relatively often looking out the window. Which is not much to look at other than the wall of the building next to this one.

My room has no bed in it either. They must not consider that I will require any sleep.

The floor is white—well, most of it anyway.

Nice and white like after snow first falls.

Worn down in places like in front of the door or where the wallpaper in three of the corners is peeled away. But not in that one corner, I thought. That one blemish stands out the most.

The ceiling has but one light bulb, hanging down low from it.

Old by the looks of it. Yellow with age.

It has no string or switch on the wall to turn it on or off—it's on now—but most of the light is coming from the window.

I decide then to walk over to the window and look out—that's when it happens.

Let me try to put my thoughts in words that even I can understand.

I could smell things—not bad smells. But remembering smells.

Like candy apples at the state fair or cotton candy.

The smell of rain on a spring night's air, and I had to sit down.

Is this why the chair is here by the window? I thought to myself.

I was overwhelmed with intoxicating odors to the point where you could taste them.

Sitting down I started to breathe easier—one breath at a time, slowly I told myself as I closed my eyes, slowly breathing through my nose.

Then they came at me again—these inhibitions forcing their way in.

The smell of an open field of wildflowers, the pages of a new book when you first open it.

The smell of grass when cut. These odors reached out to me.

My mind was in a thousand different places all at once.

I don't know how long I sat there, five minutes, ten—it could have been five hours just sitting there breathing slowly in and out.

At some time I opened my eyes to look out the window to see shadows dancing across the side of the building next to me. How long was I staring? Who knows—but the more I stared at those shadows they began to take shape.

It sounds mad I know sitting there having these overwhelming odors and now—now seeing shapes in the shadows, like children running or throwing a ball back and forth.

Someone old sitting on a park bench feeding some birds, a couple holding hands while they walked away, and I cried.

One tear from my eye—down the side of my cheek.

I let it go and breathed in deeply.

The taste of my tear when it touched my mouth brought even more smells.

How long?

How long have I been sitting? I thought to myself.

My legs hurt and my feet were starting to tingle. I wanted to get up then. Start walking around—let the blood flow through my legs.

But it's so nice—where did that come from, was that me?

This spot—it's familiar.

Looking around my room, the three corners where the wallpapers were torn.

The one wall where the door was at.

I looked at the far corner now. Dark and uninviting. But familiar just the same.

The window was too far away to cast any light on that side of the room and my one light bulb hanging down didn't seem to shed enough light either.

I closed my eyes again, and then stood up.

Feeling lightheaded. The images of the shadows still playing across my mind.

Slowly—so slowly I open my eyes again, to see that my door was open. Open!

How long? How long has it been open?

There I was standing next to the chair feeling the rush of blood going back into my legs.

How long?

I took a step towards the door—this is a dream—it's not really open.

I take another step and stop, my hands are free.

Free! For how long?

I touch my face running my hand through my hair.

My tear dried long before.

Before?

I stopped looking back out my window to see the shadows playing across the building and they're gone.

I breathe in quickly—the smells they're gone too!

How long? How long have I been standing there?

I face the door again. Open, it's open.

I walk to the door slowly taking each breath, each sight in and I stop again to look down.

The paint is worn not on the outside of the door—but inside where I'm standing.

Have I been here before?

Think—and there's that word again.

The door is open. My hands are free. Just one step and I'll be through that door.

I look back around now, I have been here before. I close my eyes again, I want to leave or do I want to stay?

With one step I walk through the door.

Eyes open most likely to come back again once more.

My friend and I finishing up our coffee only to laugh at this place of mine I've come to call Room Six . . .

I Couldn't Afford to Drink (But I Drank Anyway)

There were many times in my using that I couldn't afford what my drinking habits had become.

There was a time in the beginning that I could, really I could.

You see—starting out by acting the big shot when going into the bar, always giving over more money to the barkeep in the hope that they remembered me the next time around.

Always acting like I had "It" to give away.

Gave me the false sense of security that I seemed to need at that time.

Now don't get me wrong, there really was a time that I had the means to have "It".

Thinking what I thought was a good time—not a very long time—but it was there nevertheless.

As my using progressed so did my spending habits.

It seemed at the time if I worked more I'd get more, so I could spend more, so I worked more.

Never seeing the vicious circle my life had become.

But as I drank, the alcohol started to take more of a need to drink.

Becoming what I have found for me and heard in recovery that it was no mere habit.

I think we all have some sort of story of this behavior.

One of mine in particular stands out and this happened way before I came into recovery.

I headed out one afternoon taking the last five dollar bill off the counter of my home, knowing that that had to last 'til pay day—which was two days away.

I sat down in my favorite bar chair and had my first drink.

Trying to get my thoughts in order.

You know those priorities that we have.

The ones that stood in front of my drinking.

Telling the barkeep all my woes—how life isn't fair.

How and get this—how I didn't have enough money to get the things I needed or better yet, what I thought I deserved in life.

Just to give over the last five dollars to pay for my drinks and heading home.

Pulling into my driveway thinking—what was in the house to drink.

Trying to remember if I had any alcohol that I "placed" for that rainy day.

Getting in the house to hear that question—

"Did you pick up the milk and bread that I asked while you were out?

I saw that the money was gone off the counter top—

You didn't forget did you?"

It still amazes me how when I was in the thick of "It"—my using

—when I didn't think I affected anyone but myself, how wrong I was.

Enough time has gone by since then and I can still see the look of disappointment on my partner's face when I had lied,

—that I had forgot

—I'll be right back

—looking in vain for some change under the seats of my truck—the floor mats too.

Saying that prayer, "Just enough, please God—please be enough."

So I could afford the things that I—no—that we really needed.

I think we all have stories like this one.

This is just one of many stories of what alcohol cost me most of the time.

That I Couldn't Afford to Drink (But I Drank Anyway) . . .

Walking in my New Pair of Shoes

From the first day that I stopped using I was given what the old-timers call a toolbox.

That first day I stepped into that meeting—unbeknownst at the time I was given the

"How to stay sober spiel." "One day at a time."

Please don't get me wrong by making it sound easy—it's not—but it can be done.

How often have I heard, "It's a program for those who want it." Not a, "Program for those who need it."

If that were the case you likely would never find a seat to sit on when going to a meeting.

But upon getting that toolbox with all of the information on how to do it. Was a new pair of shoes to walk in.

Now I'm not saying that I'm walking in their shoes—but I am walking the same path as they are or did.

The ones who came before.

The ones that had no idea what was in store for them.

Not that I knew what was going to happen to me in the beginning—still don't at times.

But they can tell us what lies ahead—down the road, what to expect, what to look out for.

While walking this path of recovery.

Those first brave folks that trudged along what we call, "That happy road of destiny," while walking in their new shoes.

One day during winter time, right after that first big snowfall, I walked outside to start shoveling—not one of my favorite things to do—but I do it anyway.

I walked to the end of my driveway and turned around.

Looking back on the snow-covered driveway and seeing how my footprints look—this must be how the program looked starting out with one walking down making a path.

So I walked back through the snow making sure to step in the same footprints as before.

Stopping and looking back—the path was a little different.

Walking back through the path again to see my trail had grown just a little bit bigger.

I can see now why they told me you don't have to pave the road, it's already been done. I just have to walk on the road that started out a small trail and through the years grew to become quite a big road.

The folks that came before me paved the way.

So here I am traveling down this big lane of happy fortune. Trying to stay in the middle where it's safe and all I have to do is follow the directions the way they're laid out—oh—and change everything about myself too.

Seeing the people just ahead of me and asking for help or just behind to say watch out, to seeing what works for some—may not work for me or others.

The path or road is very wide now.

What started out as one set of footprints was turned into a small path, then into a small road to the larger highway we walk upon today.

And if I can just keep on doing the next right thing—I can stop and look around.

To take in the scenery—being okay where I am in life—to thanking my higher power for just today.

And the only real worry on this road of healing is not forgetting that I'm powerless.

Getting my life back was but the first of many miracles. Heck, even having to shovel this driveway is one.

As long as I keep on walking this road.

Be open, be willing, and so I have.

I just keep walking.

Being given new shoes for my feet is one way I like to look at it.
Starting a new way of life is just another.
One step at a time.
While walking in my New Pair of Shoes . . .

My Father's Hands

This thought came to me when I was sitting down next to my father in the hospital.

Dad was in again due to his breathing or lack of.

He had asked me to trim his fingernails for him.

As I was trimming them I saw for the first time just how old his hands looked.

All the wrinkles of time, to all the age spots showing.

I couldn't get over just how old my dad had become while lying in this hospital bed.

Looking at my own hands and seeing how they're shaping up now.

The small traces of lines forming from time—the age spots slowly being seen.

As I held my father's hands it came to me all the things his hands had held throughout these years.

From holding my grandmother's hand to his horse Major's reins to the simple thing as a cup of water to his lips.

There is history in all our hands.

From tying our first shoe laces to that first button down shirt.

I started to see the past of my father within those hands.

He would tell me about the farm he grew up on.

Those hands moved dirt and tools to farm with.

Off to war so people like me can live with freedom freely.

From holding his mother's hands to his first date.

To his wife as they started their life together.

Holding on to my brothers; then to me in the end.

His hands have felt the touch of so many things in life—that looking at them now made me realize how my life or better yet—just what my hands have touched so far in life.

My father told me once that you could tell a lot about someone with just their handshake.

To look someone in the eyes when shaking their hand meant something at one point.

That deals were done upon their word and a handshake.

How much we placed upon that.

When I started my journey in recovery who knew all the things that my hands would touch.

All those handshakes at meetings.

From being welcomed in.

To the one welcoming people in.

To see people bound with just that simple handshake.

You can see the friendships starting up that will last one day at a time.

How easily we can forget to hold on to those hands when we think it's going too bad.

Looking down at my own hands again and seeing my father's hands looking back.

Maybe not as much has touched them like my father's—but God willing they'll get there.

Trying not to forget that it all started with me holding on to that drink, thinking that my life should be so much better if only "they" would leave me alone.

Never realizing that my life was unmanageable because of that drink.

How much money passed between these hands to pay for the things that ended up destroying my life in the end.

Finishing up trimming my dad's' fingernails and really seeing for the first time just where my life was going today.

To knowing just what my hands touch on a daily basis.

The handshakes that greet us to the handshakes that binds us in life.

Being responsible in what my hands hold onto throughout today.

Working on my fathers' nails was just another God shot in how I interact with all my affairs today.

Being mindful of where I've been, to now.

As I let go of My Fathers' Hands . . .

Check

As I started my day I noticed that I was going down this mental checklist of the things needing to be done throughout the day.
It happened quite literally as something like the coffee pot was on.
Just one of the items on my checklist.
But honestly—it was as simple as that.
No great light shining over my table as I had my morning coffee.
But as I sipped my last mouthful my mind couldn't help but know that there is a light.
That understanding of my faith and knowing that I'm not alone.
So, in a sense, there is that light shining down, or more to the point, from within.
So the checklist continues, starting with waking up, not coming to—check one.
Knowing where I am—check two.
To who's beside me, super grateful for that one—check three.
Glasses on—check four.
And then on my knees so I can stand throughout the day, check—five.
To where I'm in my kitchen having coffee.
As the day progresses I'm more aware of my checklist.
The freedom of making choices, having a job, my health, my family, and friends.
Having faith in my life today.
Knowing that I'm not alone.
What a God-awful way I lived before I came into recovery.
The not knowing, or the big one I seemed to have, "Not even caring."

That feeling of no one understands, and that I'm all alone can really do a job on one's mind.

Mental, physical, and spiritual; a threefold disease.

Making those amends when they crop up.

It says in our writings when selfishness, dishonesty, resentments, and fear come upon us we should act.

Not if this should happen—but when.

Following the directions that are laid out before us.

So I continue to go down my checklist.

Staying sober—check.

Staying mindful—check.

Not taking my self so damn seriously—check, check, and check.

Knowing my limitations and strengths.

Learning to, as they say—"let it go."

To a gratitude list as the day goes by.

So by the end of the day I'm sitting on the side of my bed, being filled with the happiness of, "Freedom of self."

Then on my knees so I can sleep right tonight, thanking my higher power for just today, just for today.

I close my eyes and thank God for the willingness to live today.

That I'm sober and aware of all the things on my checklist.

"As I get back out of bed, head down the stairs, and into the kitchen.

So I can turn off the coffee pot!"

Check . . .

Once Upon a Line

Once upon a line it seemed that no matter how much I had—I still wanted more.

Once upon a line I heard that I didn't need anyone to feel all alone.

There was a time where I had to wait in lines.

Lines at the bank or the gas station—even when young there were lines in the school cafeteria just for some food.

All in the name of fun I would wait in line—sitting around the bar table looking at people that I didn't know waiting for the barkeep to bring me my next drink.

Looking at my reflection in the mirror staring back at me.

Walking on that fine thin line of insanity and sane.

Having small glimpses of reality come through my head on what to do next.

There always was a line somewhere.

The line to stand in when I was going to that new club.

Starting out looking so cool to being so washed up by the end of the night.

Flushing the toilet with the tips of my boots, just to be sitting there backwards making lines 'til 2:00 am.

Like most fairy tales this one starts off just the same with one exception: it's real.

As we start our story we come upon a young man waiting in the line at the bank.

As he starts getting closer to the teller thinking just give me my money, he starts feeling the overpowering thoughts of when he gets out of this line, what it's going to take to get to his dealer's house to get his fix.

The power of using is starting to run through his veins like he was already high.

As the bank teller counts out his money he thinks just for a moment that rent is due, never stopping and thinking that he still owes his dealer for that last fix he got the other day. Not once thinking that there's still no heat in the apartment or any food.

Why would he.

Once the thought of using enters his mind he's off and running.

Never stopping to think what's wrong with this.

At that time—nothing is wrong.

After he sees his dealer and pays him off, just to be fronted some more he heads home.

Sneaking by his landlord's open door to that stairway with that one creaking step.

Opening his door ever so slowly to not hear it squeak.

Over to lighting a candle for some ambience and maybe some heat.

Looking around his small room for the things that he needs.

Never stopping to see the destruction he is making as his head comes closer to that first line.

Sitting back and wondering how he's going to get more.

Blowing out his candle he sees his breath in the air. No heat will do that.

Opening his door ever so slowly to peek down the hall.

Listening in vain for any sound coming up from downstairs.

Over that one creaking step and heading outside.

When did it become day time? He thinks to himself—what day is it anyway?

Down the street to try to score some more.

Asking passersby's if they have any loose change or a few bucks to spare, to seeing an old man sitting down in the shade by the side of a building holding a sign that reads will work for food.

Looking down to say, "I'll never be him—man, that's got to stink—there's got to be help for that guy somewhere.

He's just got to stand in the right line.

Get some help and move on with his life."

As the old man looks up too tired to try—saying to our young passerby—

"I was just like you once, never stopping to see the destruction I made to myself or to others who cared.

I had a purpose in life too—'til I started down this road so many years ago.

I was just like you, always looking for more and look where it got me, all washed up and poor."

"Yah, you." He says as our man just keeps walking down the road.

As the old man lowers and shakes his head.

I could hear him say,

"I had a life too.

"I was just like you—Once Upon a Line." . . .

Mexican Apple Pie

Here's a story of my Dad's cooking gone bad.

The morning started out the same for the last couple of days.

Dad, knowing where he was and who he was—not a big deal to some—if you know that—but Dad has been forgetting a lot lately due to getting older.

The church had given us some apples early this week—just because, well, that's what they do—just—you know what I mean.

Anyway, seeing the apples on the counter as I was making my lunch gave me an idea.

"Dad, would you peel and slice the apples so I can make a pie after work?"

"Sure." Dad said.

"Just set them out on the counter." He added.

"They're on the counter already." I said.

"No, they're in the refrigerator." He says.

"No, they're on the counter." I say.

"Are you sure?" Dad asked.

"Pretty sure, Dad." Not telling him that I was looking right at them in front of me.

"Well, just make sure they're out so I can peel them." He says.

"Yah, pa. I will." I said.

Like I said earlier, Dad tends to forget.

On coming home I went to the refrigerator to get some water.

Looking down I noticed a pan covered with aluminum foil—not that that was a surprise.

It seems we always have bowls and platters but no covers.

The day I open the package of plastic wear the covers must be getting thrown out along with all the wrappings.

None can be found.

Maybe I should ask Dad—nah.

"Thanks Dad for slicing up the apples." I say as I closed the refrigerator door.

Going into the living room where Dad was watching T.V. he says.

"Did you see what I did?"

"Yah. Thanks." I said.

"No." He says.

"I made the pie." He adds.

Oh God. I thought.

"Well." Said I.

"I was going to get the stuff to make it tonight at the store."

"We had the stuff in the refrigerator." He says.

"We did?" I ask.

"Yes. Don't you ever look?" He says over the T.V . . .

Yah, but we had no cinnamon. I thought to myself.

"You know you've got to look around sometimes to see what we have to work with."

He pipes in.

"Yah, pa, you're right." I say.

Feeling like I just stepped into a bad Abbott and Costello skit. Who's on first deal.

After supper, Dad sitting back in his chair, my partner handing him a piece of pie along with one for himself—please don't ask why I didn't get one—that's a story for a different time—those who know my partner—just know.

Anyway, out from the kitchen I hear,

"What the heck is this?" My partner asked.

"Is what?" I ask.

"What I'm eating." He says.

"I don't know? I don't have ESP." I say.

"Is this supposed to be apple pie?" He says out loud.

"Yes, for Pete's sake. I made that today." Dad says.

"You did?" Is his response.

"Yes—why does no one believe that I can still cook around here?" He yells over the T.V . . .

"Well, I thought we had no cinnamon." I told him.

"Oh, for goodness sake.

Am I the only one who looks around the house to make stuff to eat?" He says.

"No." My partner said.

"I usually look around the kitchen if I'm going to cook something. Not the whole house." He points out.

Once again I'm back in that Abbott and Costello skit.

"What's in this?" He asked.

"Apples!" Dad yells over the T.V . . .

"Yah, I know that. But what are these little brown pieces? And why's it so hot?" He asks.

"It's hot from cooking." Dad says.

"It is? Well, what time did you make it?" My partner asked.

Dad, once again yelling over the television, "This morning. Then I put it in the refrigerator." Why he says.

"So it's been in the fridge at least five hours and it's still hot?" He asks.

"I don't know why?" He shoots back.

Looking over at my father as I picked up his plate I say.

"Dad, just what did you put in the pie?"

"The stuff from the fridge." He said.

"What stuff?" (i.e.—on the word stuff—let me clarify—that could be anything that ends up in the refrigerator—eggs, soda, socks). I asked.

Going over to the counter where the pie now sits, taking a small mouthful, I realized it is hot and looking very red.

"Is there hot sauce in this thing?" My partner says from the table.

My God, there is hot sauce in this. I thought to myself.

"Dad, what did you make the apple pie with?" I yell from the kitchen.

"Oh, I'm getting really tried of you two thinking I can't cook." He yells back.

"No one said that Dad." I'm just asking.

Going over to the table hearing my Dad yelling.

"Fine! I'll never cook again." He says real load.

To hearing my partner saying,

"Fine! You're banned from cooking."

And me, waiting for that 50's show music to start playing do do do do.

Thinking, this is my life.

Oh God, this is my life.

Going over to my partner to get his plate.

"Here let me throw that away." I said.

"Throw what away?" He says.

"The pie!" I say.

"It's gone." He replies.

"Gone?" I asked.

"Yah." He tells me.

"Where?" I asked.

"I ate it." He tells me.

"You did?" I reply.

"Yah." He says with a weird look on his face.

"But I thought you didn't like it?" I ask.

"I didn't." He says.

"But you ate it?" I tell him.

"I was hungry." He says while walking away from me.

Like I said, Dad sometimes forgets and apparently so does my partner. Oh, and before I forget . . . here's the new recipe in our house.

Poppoes' Mexican Apple Pie

1 Bag crab apples
Peeled and sliced
Wash with dish soap until bubbles are gone
Place in pie bowl—cover not needed
Add sugar to taste
1 large tablespoon salt
1 dash over shoulder
A handful of bacon bits
2 dashes of hot sauce
2 more for coloring
Bake in oven @ 700 degrees
For 5 minutes
Or until hot sauce bubbles

P.S. Come to think of it—serve in hard Taco shell with a two finger scoop of whipped cream or ice cream on the side—for your very own piece of Mexican Apple Pie . . .

Here Today

Now that some time has gone by—enough where I can put my thoughts into words—of the experience that happened, not just to me, but the small group of us, and what happened to a young man that I will never know.

I ask myself why this happened.

I've asked myself how could this have happened.

I'd like to think that if there were some way to turn back time—to see just enough into the future that this would not have happened.

Taking another road, leaving just a little bit earlier from our job site.

That this wouldn't have happened. But it did.

What started out as just an ordinary day—sure ended up being one of the most hair-raising days of my life.

Not just in my sobriety. But in life.

I've written a lot of short stories on what my life in and out of sobriety has been.

The choices I've made, good or bad. The choices I see people make around me in and out of the of recovery.

The right ones, the not so great ones and then there are the truth ones.

Ones that just are.

We make them every day. How we interact with others. How we hold up under stress.

To giving ourselves the chance to change.

I've never met this young man but I know that the chance for change is done with him.

From that day forward his journey is over on this plane of existence.

How can this not affect me or the people I was with?

How can this not affect the family and friends of that young man?
It can't. It won't.
It will always be there—especially the family—some close friends.
For me, as time passes—the event will subside—some, hopefully. I don't know.
This is a first for me.
The first twenty-four hours was something. The dreams of that young man sitting up with all of us standing around him.
To the van that I was driving with the clients from my company rolling over and over, instead of off to the side of the road, has played out in my head the first few days.
Talking to other people helps—some.
Oh, I've talked to the police, the fireman, and the insurance companies. Even the local newspaper.
"What did you see?" They all ask.
To saying, "What a shame."
A life should not be summed up by those three words.
But that's what it is.
I've been sober long enough to know it isn't God. That's one thing I'm very grateful to have known.
Yah, sure I've asked God why—how the heck could I not. Praying for the family, to praying and saying thanks that it wasn't one of the clients I'm responsible for.
To even saying why not me instead of an eighteen year old, that to me has his whole life ahead of him.
My friends say, "That's life.
These things happen all the time. It just happened to be you."
The road we were on was as busy as any other during that week.
Not too much traffic for that time of day. The road wasn't wet or covered with snow and the traffic was going at the average speed.
Heading north when we were struck. One second nothing—the next he was in our lane, hitting the side of our vehicle.
Like I said, "No reason."
Being able to keep the van from rolling, to thinking we're going to go over the ravine, in what seemed like minutes were just seconds.
Having the clients all in shock and trying to get out so I could find out what happened, to actually seeing the extent of the damage to us and the pile of wreckage on the highway.

Hearing the screams for help to see the best and worst of people.

The ones that stopped and helped.

The ones that just drove by.

Can't really blame them, I don't even know if I would've stopped.

I would like to believe or think I would have.

There was a time within my cups of using that I would've told you that I did.

"The Hero."

These are the moments in life when you just don't know 'til it happens.

That road we're on in life has all those moments.

I remember when my foster son passed away, to holding the hand of my mother. Seeing that last moment go by.

As time moved on with these moments, those memories I've taken comfort in believing that they are in a better place. That God has called them home.

I've come to believe that there is a place and still work to be done on a higher plane of existence.

I remember that day when our country was devastated—how we all as a nation looked on in horror. I remember saying to my Dad at the time that my foster son David and my mother were very busy ushering home the lost souls on this road of life.

I don't know if that's the right way to think, but it helps.

Believing that my God works through other people.

Call them angels or what I like to think of them as agents of God.

Taking comfort in that small way helps.

I like to think that this young man is now busy working for God—ushering the men, women, and children that pass away every day.

To know and attempt to take some comfort with that.

Life moves on for us. On any road we are on.

Be it early recovery, newly married, new job or new town or city we end up at to live our lives. Any of those firsts we have in life.

We will all have the chance to change—one day at a time, if we choose to.

When all this happened I intuitively surrounded myself with the people that are doing what it takes to live happy, sober, and somewhat a sane life.

Hearing again that we can't live in yesterday, that tomorrow is yet to come.

That any chance of change is done now. It's not what you leave behind, it's how you lived through life that people remember.

For in the end, we are all just Here Today . . .

Fishing in the Soup Bowl

Get a grip, someone told me once when I started telling my side of the story.

Still talking to that half-way point 'til my brain catches up to what was said to me.

Mouth hanging open. Think—did they just tell me to get a grip?

What the heck was that.

Where did that come from?

I mean I know where—the person right in front of me, but the comment—get a grip.

Seeing the last 24 hours, hell, the last week playing over and over in my mind like some screwed up projector playing one of those films that always skipped that I remembered from school.

The ones like "The salmon swim upstream to mate, overcoming great obstacles—including death." Or "When you hear the sirens—fall under your desk with your hands over your head." Yah, that would stop the blast.

But get a grip.

I'm hanging here by the seat of my pants and all they can tell me is, "Get a grip." I say.

"Yah—that's what I said, oh, and breathe." They tell me.

"What?" I ask again.

"Breathe." They tell me again.

"You've been holding your breath." They added.

"I have." I said.

God. I have, haven't I? I think to myself.

When I was talking to them I was explaining how in the beginning I was looking for the easy way out, telling them when I started fishing in the soup bowl of life I'm bound to end up with something I'd rather not.

Every time I said something to my sponsor he would give me a suggestion and I would say to him sure, then go find someone I could explain myself to—cause obviously he didn't understand what I was saying.

Every time I start looking for something in life—new car—new job, even a new hair cut—I always found something different.

It seemed I always fished something else out of the soup bowl.

My father was a cook—so I heard many times how too many hands in the broth could spoil the stew.

Never really paying too much attention to that, even when I came into a program.

'Til I started down this journey of recovery. Always going to too many people for the answer that I should've taken by my sponsor in the first place.

But that's not how it worked out for me. I'm not the poster boy for the program. I'll leave that up to the ones that seem to like the lime light.

For me it was like every time I'd go out to get, I don't know, say a belt, I'd walk out with a job.

Going out to get my hair cut and being in a twelve car pileup and a fancy new leg brace to boot.

Always something different than what I was fishing for.

Just the other day I was with some friends and one of them asked when did I know that I was powerless over my life. Oh, that's easy I told them.

When the path of destruction I left behind started to catch up to me.

We all laughed at that. You know this is the only place that I've known that when we share about how bad our lives were we all pretty much nod or smile.

Sometimes laughing at some of the worst things I've ever heard while out there—using. Sometimes bad things happen—not a lot of people nodded or smiled, some—well, most were horrified that I would even be talking about it.

Let alone be laughing at it.

To them I was the oddity.

To the folks in recovery—I was just another clown on the bus.

Even in sobriety I have found that I still can go fishing in the soup. Throwing my line out—seeing the bobber go up and down—thinking I'll get a nice chunk of meat when I would pull out a soggy piece of carrot.

When I'm not taking my sponsors' advice and I'm looking for that out—the easier, softer way at the time. Going to two or three different people fishing for that answer that I wanted right along. That's when I was in trouble.

The soup has many flavors and many ingredients, too.

You'll think I'd know by now not to go looking—but just let it happen. God's time—not mine.

Well, it's easy to say the words, but to put them into practice is another thing entirely. How often did I set out in doing something and always looking for the result that was going to be—just what I wanted?

How often did I set up the game board of life—to make sure I would win?

Always fishing.

When I think of all the times I spent on making me look good. The results were just the same. People will always judge by actions, not intentions.

As soon as that came around for me, things started to get better.

As long as I stopped Fishing in the Soup Bowl . . .

Never, Never Prayer

I don't know how many times I've used this prayer.

Probably more times then I care to think about, never mind being honest about it.

What I never even knew was that's what I was doing when I was using it. As far back as I can think it was there.

Being told to, "Wake up—it's time for school." Rolling over and pulling the sheets over my head, to hoping my Mom didn't come back in—she did and it turned out worse than the first time.

Should've gotten up on time looking back now and seeing that small young man saying, "When I grow up I'll never have to do this again." And when I got older that's just what I did.

I stopped, never looking back. 'Til I came into the program and started to change.

Not finishing school was just one of the beginnings that were a long train of wreckage in my life.

Being late for work and having my boss tell me—"One more time, we start at 6:30 around here. Don't be late again."

I can still see me saying, "Absolutely, never, never again."

Well, I lost that job too—but it wasn't because of me. They just didn't see the bigger picture that was my life.

But you know they did—by trying to help me, and I shut the door on their faces.

You'll never see me again—boasting as I walked out the door.

I can't even tell you how many times I swore that I'd never get high any more, never having any fronted to me, never get behind the wheel to go home from the bar that was two streets from my home.

Didn't I say that I could just walk?

Never seeing the look on my Mom's face as she stood in the door—looking out at me. Thinking—"Would you just go back in. You're embarrassing me."

As I would get into my friend's car looking for more.

Before she passed away she told me that she prayed to God that—and get this—"The never, never prayer."

"Please may I never get that phone call." She told me.

I know today that that prayer doesn't have to be said by someone like me in recovery.

People often tell me that they have used this type of prayer, too.

There are those that I worked with that don't even know about me, that I hear them saying those same never prayers.

Telling their bosses that they'll never be late.

Saying to co-workers could'ya just tell them I stayed 'til 4:00, and I have to laugh at myself—cause truly there I am—staring right back at myself.

Seeing my friends come in on Monday—late and looking like I did—and all I can say is, "Never, never again. Please God." And go about my day. Hoping for the best.

I've been in the program now for over ten years and Mom's been gone almost ten years, too. I can still see her lying in bed as we talked about life—having her tell me, no, saying to me, "Never have I been so proud of you."

Seeing now that that prayer isn't always used to getting me out of trouble.

Seeing it used with faith today.

I hope to God that I never lose sight of that.

Just one of the lessons I've learned and still try to apply when my defects pop up.

Never taking this disease for granted.

Seeing too many folks just giving up.

May I never get to that point where the pain is so great that I won't want to use that prayer?

We all have our bottoms—we all have our way of saying our prayers—and I know I have a lot of yets'.

But it's the agains' that bring me to my knees.

Asking God's help.

For the strength with my Never, Never Prayer . . .

Colors

Most of us have seen a rainbow at least once in our lives and a few sunsets on a hot summer's day.

I can still hear my parents say, "Don't look directly into the sun."

But I did—now waiting for those sun spots to dissipate. Should've listened—but I had to find out for myself. Like most things in life.

Oh, sure I've been told by my parents to do certain things, like hold on to my hand while waiting for the lights to turn from green to red so we could walk across the street. Like most, I've seen colors since I was born; I'm very lucky for that.

But it's not 'til I came into a program on recovery that I really started to see.

There was a time when I was taught about colors. Not just the simple color wheel, but the colors of life and I'm not saying the colors of people either.

My mother was a big influence with me with colors. "Seeing beyond the surface." She'd say. Looking at the whole picture or at least trying to today.

Most people don't even see the colors of living, too caught up in their daily lives; and when you see it, it's usually due to the negative things we see or hear about.

Those people—what a shame. We then see the colors, don't we—including me.

How often I hear in life, "Are you blue." "So mad I can see red."

"Green with envy." Or "White as a ghost."

Even as a young man trying to fit in with the crowd—hearing, "I dare yah, what are yah, chicken, you must be yellow."

So I would do whatever they asked so I could fit in.

Now in recovery I try to see the colors of life that are helpful to me.

Hearing in the meeting that I attended, "Stay green." Hearing about that, "Pink cloud." And hearing, "How dark resentments can make one drink."

You could almost see how black that thought pattern is.

I'd hear, "I was beat up 'til I was black and blue from using."

But as time goes by I'm starting to see what my Mom was trying to tell me.

"Don't judge a book by its cover; don't judge a person just by their appearance."

Most people can't or maybe even won't see the colors around them and I'm not talking about someone who's blind.

I have a friend who's blind and he tells me about colors all the time. He tells me that they're beautiful to look at, and I shake my head, thinking that most people even with 20/20 vision won't see how beautiful they are.

I hear, "Stay with the winners." "Not hanging out at the old haunts."

Those black places of my mind.

Do these things have color? Maybe not ones I can see—but the ones that I can feel.

When I know today that I'm doing something that I'm not too sure about, I feel bad, sick—brindle brown. Feeling low—being blue.

Doing something for someone without them knowing it or for the ones that we love.

Feeling happy, content—being red as roses.

To finding that silver lining in those storm clouds of life.

When I started this journey the only color I seemed to see was black—well, maybe gray, due to the drinking and using 'til I started the steps to change.

What I thought was a light at the end of the tunnel didn't turn out to be the headlight of the train coming at me, but the light of day on this seemingly, hopeless life.

When the change started to happen, so did my awareness of the colors around me.

Seeing with new eyes it seems, when I looked at life and all its beautiful Colors . . .

Good morning, God

Good morning, God, it's me, but you probably already know that.

Well, come to think of it—you most likely do.

So what this is, is a formality on my part I guess.

I just got up from bed and was heading to the shower to get my day started, when it came to me that I haven't said good morning to you yet.

So let's start my day on my knees, so I can stand up for the day ahead.

I have to tell you—what a night I had last night.

Don't know how long it's been since I stayed out that late. It's been awhile and I couldn't find my shoe before I went to bed, oh well.

God, I humbly ask you to remove the desire to drink and drug away from me.

Please, Lord, remove the desire to eat compulsively away also. Or buy any scratch tickets.

Lord, may I do your will and not my own.

I ask you for the help today because I can't do it on my own.

A grateful heart will never drink or drug or overeat, I hear.

So I want to be grateful.

Lord, I've made a mess of this life; please help me with today so I can live as a free person.

God, give me the strength to do your will.

Since I haven't even gotten off of my knees yet and while I still have your attention, could you please look out for the ones that I love and care for?

Oh, God, here I am asking you to do all these things and I haven't even started my day yet. Okay, okay let's start this over.

Help me with the things I already asked for and help me stay out of my own way.

Oh boy, that doesn't sound any better now, does it.

God, that must sound like I'm telling you what to do, which I'm not, well, I am come to think about it, but that's not what I mean. It is, but not like that.

Okay, I think I've got myself into a repeating loop, but you know what I mean, right?

I mean you're God, right?

What am I saying of course you know you're you, right?

I just didn't want it to sound like I was telling you what to do.

But asking.

No, that's not right either, it is, but isn't.

This is a lot harder than I thought it would be and my knees are starting to hurt.

How can I be grateful with the thought of pain in my legs?

Well, it's not really a thought—the pain is there.

Oh boy, here I go again.

Should I be grateful that there's pain in my legs and that my feet have fallen to sleep.

I mean you know this already, right? Anyhow, I'm just saying if you're not too busy helping me through the day—whatever that will be and if you have a moment—could you please look in on the folks that I love and care for.

That would be great.

Oh yah, one more thing.

Thank you for a good night's sleep.

Even though I didn't really sleep that well.

I did a lot of tossing and turning through the night and I think I had too much tonic before I went to bed.

I had to get up and use the bathroom twice. Not that I'm not grateful for the bathroom or that I woke up in time to go.

God knows what a mess that would've been. Well, I guess you would have, wouldn't you.

Or that I even acknowledge that I have a bed to sleep on and not a patch of grass outside my home or someplace else that I would come to and play that game, "Where's that ceiling."

Not that I wouldn't be grateful, just not very comfortable.

I mean I would still be okay with it,

I hope,

I didn't think so.

No, really, I guess I would be doing it my own way if that happens, so please help me not to make those kinds of choices.

Great. Here I go again asking you for more help when you probably have enough on your plate to deal with already.

I mean, I think you do.

I mean, I would.

No, that's not what I mean.

I mean if I were you, not that I want to be you, God.

God, no.

Whoops. Sorry.

That's what got me into trouble in the first place, acting like you.

When all I had to do was ask for help.

Boy, this is harder than I thought it would be and I can't feel my feet anymore.

Is it hot in here?

Should I be grateful for that, too?

I think I would like to start this over again. 'Cause you probably know most of what I said, I mean ask for.

Thank God I'm alone, where no one can see me like this.

Not that I would be ashamed to have anyone look at me now that I'm on the floor.

What's that saying when you start at the bottom there's only one way to go and that's up?

But boy, do I wish someone was around now to help me off the floor.

Oh, so that's where my other shoe went, thought I looked under my bed, come to think about it I did, didn't I?

I guess I do have a lot to be grateful for, now that I'm off the floor with both of my shoes. All I really should've said to you is, thank you and Good morning, God . . .

Life & Reality Collide

As I was putting these short stories together I started to see a pattern within them.

One that should have been obvious to me—but then again I'm still learning.

My sponsor would laugh at that, so wouldn't my friends at work.

But I am trying.

My life as a sober alcoholic and the everyday realties that I face are very different today because I'm sober.

How often I would play out—say an event in my head, "This is how it's going be." Only to have it end much, much differently.

What a mess my life became when those thoughts and actions collided.

We hear, "You have a thinking problem today." And that's so true. Hearing, "Get a checkup from the neck up." That one's true, too, for me

When I start trying to take over and plan on the outcome then I'm in a danger zone.

Looking for different results to the same problems always collided.

From how one should do it. To it's none of my business. To taking over or giving it over.

Living in the solution—not the problem. Things just seemed to work out better.

Better for me and definitely better for the folks around me.

Waking up—no I mean coming to, thinking today's going to be different.

But not doing a bloody thing different to make it happen, always collided.

How many times I'd pray to God to, "Please, please make it go away."
Only to take my will back—mad and upset that life was treating me unfairly.
Pushing God away because he wasn't doing what I "told" him he should be doing.
Thinking that I should be making more money—"I can't pay my bills."
Not taking the responsibility that most—if not all that I made was going to my using back then. Hearing my employers tell me, "We have overtime available."
Just to tell them, "Oh no, not this weekend, I'm way too busy."
Knowing damn well that all I was doing was a big fat nothing.
I just wanted to be left alone so I could drink and drug.
I've met a woman that helped me understand the importance of, "When your words and your actions are dissimilar nothing happened differently, when they are at the same level things start to change."
Being sober for what may be eighteen months and whining about my life I was told, "When you are ready to do the program the way it's laid out and not your way, things just might be different."
How mad I was thinking, "I was doing the steps, wasn't I, reading them off the wall—what more do you want."
Well, the reality is a lot, when I was finely ready to change.
Being accountable for my sobriety was up to me.
Half measures or you get out what you put in was just some of the reality talk that they told me as I started doing the work on myself.
It's always the times when I'm trying to drive the bus, instead of just going for the ride in life is when Life and Reality Collide . . .

Acknowledgments:

But for the grace of God there are so many people I would like to thank.

If it wasn't for anonymity, I would be shouting out peoples' names all over the place.

But for those folks that I can't give out their names and there's a lot.

Thank you.

Thank you so very, very much, for helping me along on this journey so far.

My thoughts and prayers are forever grateful to you all.

For those that inherited nick-names that we like to hand out and people I can thank openly,

here we go.

Biker Bruce, Mac O, Simon says, B, Tommy too Macho, Uncle Billy, Auntie Rob, Sister Chris, Daisy Duke Sue, In & out Jeff, Blinky, Boo Hoo Donna, John the Cable Guy, Spot, Taz,

Tea cup Jim, Angel, yard-sailing Zombies, Demon Child, Auntie Claire, Coco Pop,

Jeffie Pop, Colonel Pop, Tie your shoe Bob, Zee, Retro Girl, B.G., Mama Leona, Sunshine, Scary Shari, Patrisimo, Mountain Woman, Flipper, Bright Eyes, Pocahontas, Stud Puppet, Paris,

Mayor McCheese, Big Bob, Foo Foo Ka Choo, The Chad, Laughing Linda, Crazy Ann, Me Me, Red, Head wound Harry, Joey bag of Donuts, Psycho Fairy, Too smart Dan, Big Mike,

Little Mike, Mikie, Air force Jim, Furbie, Jeri the Chick, Incredible Dick, Sir Porch a Lot,

Sweet Tits, Little Miss, Capt. Cranky, Tuggs, Shelly, Showtime, D, Chatty Kathee, Trouble, Meat, Thelma & Louise, Mr. Spock, Bike Mike, my adopted daughter Dirty Bed Knob,

Nickey Do, Cha, Annie Banannie, Smiling Willow, Geezer, Painter Nate, Twinkie, Frisky,

Baby Gigi, Little Dave, Eye Candy, Billy Boy, Sonsonite, Bad Frank, Good Frank,

Where's Frank?, Hooker, DeManda, Booobs, God Bob, Bang your head Lucy, Mr. G.O.N.E., Run Joey Run, my Cat, Ellie May, Wifey, Blondie, all my Dominions, the walking Dead,

David Do, Big Daddy Yum Yum, Queenie and Poppoe. And in a statement I often say,

"My spirituality is not the same as yesterday. A week ago. A year ago. It can't be. It's always changing. It has to. As I continue to grow and trust in God, one moment at a time."

The End. For Now . . .

Clean up:
12:34am 10/8/2012
Second clean up:
4:17pm 12/19/2012
Last clean up
3:15am 2/13/2013